AI-POWERED SUCCESS

A Guide For Small Businesses
To Make Better Decisions
About AI Products

Helen McCandless

BALAB AUSTRALIA

BALAB AUSTRALIA

First published by BALAB Australia 2023

DISCLAIMER: As stated by law, we can not and do not make any guarantees about your ability to get results or earn any money with our ideas, information, programs or strategies. The scenarios described within are hypothetical and provided for educational purposes only. Your results will vary and depend on many factors ...including but not limited to your background, experience, and work ethic. All business entails risk as well as massive, consistent effort and action. If you're not willing to accept that, please DO NOT BUY THIS BOOK.

NATIONAL LIBRARY OF AUSTRALIA

A catalogue record for this book is available from the National Library of Australia

ISBN 978-0-646-87943-7 (Paperback)

For all the small business owners and solopreneurs
who keep the dreams of possibility alive.

A lot of people are afraid to say what they want.

That's why they don't get what they want.

\- Madonna

CONTENTS

Do not follow where the
path may lead.

Go instead where there
is no path,
and leave a trail.

\- Ralph Waldo Emerson

PREFACE

It's May 2023 as I write this book and everywhere I look there are advertisements, articles, webinars, podcasts, social media posts and news items about Artificial Intelligence, or AI as it's more commonly known.

I find the explosion of AI products exciting but also daunting. On the one hand we're being told that the "brave new world" is here and to rejoice, but then we're told that AI will be make us redundant in the blink of an eye.

This polarisation of views exists, and of course, the nay-sayers are shouting loudly, so much so that I fear that blind panic will override common sense and human ingenuity.

What to believe?

Well, there's one thing for sure - that AI technology is here and is going to play a bigger part in our lives every day. I'm a practical person and so have decided to take the view of: *Let's learn a bit about AI, see what it has to offer, what the problems are and how we can improve our lives using it, without ruining society.*

Let me tell you a story about how I got to this way of thinking...

When the AI marketing hype cycle began I was like everyone else, a little starry-eyed and hopeful. I wasn't completely convinced though, because I've worked in the Information Technology industry for over 25 years as a Senior Business Analyst and have seen new technologies come and go.

My role has been to work with new technical solutions, helping over 100 businesses to pick the right software/hardware and implement it.

And so, I thought nothing would surprise me in the IT world, but I was wrong. As I investigated the latest AI products in the marketplace, like ChatGPT, Canva's Magic Write and Stan.Store's Stanley creative assistants I saw possibilities for business that I had only hoped for in earlier technologies.

In time, the hype cycle moved to Gartner's "*Trough of Disillusionment*" where my elation was replaced by a more practical approach. I read articles and listened to podcasts talking about the issues with AI copyright, data scraping without permission or acknowledgement, AI bugs and unintended data breaches by companies who didn't realise that they should have been more careful.

"AI is a potential minefield for business", I thought.

But, a minefield with diamonds just under the surface.

How could we safely harvest those diamonds without getting hurt?

Luckily, working out business requirements and matching them to new technology solutions is one of my core skills. I've spent over 10,000 hours evaluating business processes, needs and software features so that businesses could flourish.

I could see that a world of hurt was potentially coming for business, instead of the "brave new world" being promised.

Without a basic understanding of AI, businesses could become defenceless prey to anyone peddling AI products.

I remember, oh so well in 2015, how I watched a group of senior IT executives, returning from a vendor presentation on cloud computing, with a skip in their step, telling us all that this was the way of the future, and that it would be free!

Well, we all know how that story turned out, and are still paying the bills...

AI marketing is already sounding like this, with introductory free offers, but the free product has limited functionality. If you want to have the "good stuff", then you have to pay - and the price will rise once you're locked in.

I see some amazing benefits for small business and solopreneurs, like myself, through the use of AI products. There are obvious time savings, improved customer service, quality enhancements, and assistance with creative writing tasks in sales and marketing. Not to mention the hard core data analytics that before now were only available to big players, with deep pockets.

I've discovered that the secret to safely harvesting the "field of diamonds" is to become an "Informed Customer".

In this context, *Informed Customers* are businesspeople who have a basic understanding of AI and follow a reliable method to evaluate new AI products against their own business needs.

They are people who feel confident that they can measure the true Return on Investment (ROI) on new AI products installed in their business.

Does this sound hard to achieve?

Yes.

Is it impossible?

Definitely not!

Discovering the great opportunities which exist with AI for small business and solopreneurs is worth a little effort, don't you think?

I do.

Use this book to improve your understanding about AI and benefit from this game-changing technology. I've taken the time to dive into a range of AI products, even using some of them to source technical details about how AI works, so that your transition to being an *Informed Customer* is as painless as possible.

Today is the start of your journey into the amazing world of business AI.

Let's dive in, shall we?

Helen

ICONS USED IN THIS GUIDE

As we take this exciting journey together, keep an eye out for the road signs I've created throughout the book. They've been designed to help guide you quickly to useful advice, checklists and activities.

My Notes - Lined pages to write in your ideas, questions and action items.

Quick tips for a particular section.

Activity Template - Designed for you to complete an activity based on the past chapter. You're welcome to make a reasonable number of photocopies of these pages to complete the exercises.

Checklist.

AI Basics You Need To Know - The core types of Artificial Intelligence are explained, in an easy to understand way.

Small business and AI.

Advantages of AI for small business.

Common concerns small business owners have about AI and suggested strategies for dealing with them.

ICONS USED IN THIS GUIDE

Lessons I've personally learned from working with AI products.

Top tips on how a chatbot can supercharge your business.

The 5-Step Business AI Booster Process.

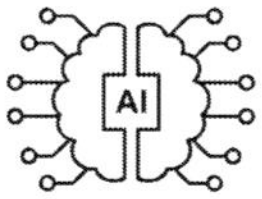

Important factors to consider when you're thinking about buying an AI product.

Especially useful features to look for in AI that is great for sales and marketing tasks.

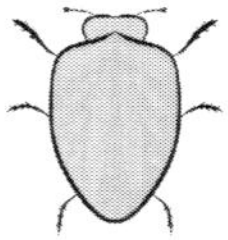

Common AI bugs.

How to measure the return on investment (ROI) on your installed AI product.

Glossary with lots of useful explanations for AI terms. Also used for the Index and Reference sections.

INTRODUCTION

Small business is starting to see the value of using Artificial Intelligence (AI) to improve sales and marketing, automate repetitive tasks, and make data-driven decisions. AI has become an increasingly popular technology, but choosing the right AI product for your business can be intimidating and expensive. This book is intended to help you make the right choice with the facts you need at hand.

Please understand that my intention here is not to make you an AI specialist, instead, to feel a level of comfort about the topic when you are meeting a potential AI supplier.

In Chapter 1 I'll walk you through the basics of AI, looking at: machine learning, natural language processing and robotics. Each has a detailed summary and a fun story which tells how that AI type can be used in everyday life. Following is a list of the most common AI types used for sales and marketing tasks. You might want to bookmark that!

Chapter 2 is a collection of stories about how small business could use AI, that I've asked some well-known AI products to create. You'll quickly pick up that AI wrote them - My main aim here is to give you some ideas about how you could use AI products in your own business. I've tried to make the selection as broad as possible, so that you'll find out how small businesses like a financial planner, an author, a bookseller, a real estate agent or a high-ticket coach might use AI to improve performance.

In Chapter 3 we'll take a look at the advantages of AI for small business before diving into the common concerns they have about using AI in Chapter 4. Each concern discussed includes a section of suggested strategies that you might like to explore.

Chapter 5 includes 15 things that I've learned in my own small business journey with AI... Some obvious and some not so, like the ease of thinking that an AI product has feelings... who would have thought? Following that is Chapter 6 with some hot tips on how chatbots can supercharge your business. Another not-to-be-missed section!

Chapter 7 explains my ***5-Step Business AI Booster Process***. This process gives you the exact steps you'll need to choose the right AI product for your business. There are activities to complete together with full instructions, to help you along the way. By the end of this chapter you'll be miles ahead of your fiercest competitors, just in business capability knowledge alone!

Chapter 8 then looks at the business factors that a Small Business Owner needs to consider when looking at AI products. These include: accuracy, scalability, privacy and transparency, just to name a few. I also delve into some uncommon factors that are important to consider before making a purchase decision.

Don't miss the Final Checklist in Chapter 9, that covers off everything you need to have in place before buying that oh so attractive AI product.

Chapter 10 is background information, listing the specific features you need to look for to get the best AI product for Sales and Marketing processes, while Chapter 11 talks about the common bugs (problems) found in all types AI and common preventative measures.

To round it all off, Chapter 12 is about the good stuff - measuring the performance of your new shiny AI product. You can even do some preliminary sums BEFORE you install it - Giving you even more reassurance about your purchase decision!

But please don't worry, I've written this chapter from a business person's perspective, not an accountant's - It's a wise idea though to get your calculations checked by a professional before making any firm decisions. The Return on your Investment into AI is important to your business profitability, so take the time to be sure about buying an AI product.

Some administrative matters:
I recommend that you read this book from the beginning to the end because I've designed each chapter to introduce new concepts while building on the information provided in the earlier chapters.

Please understand that this is a workbook, not a textbook, so I've added extra pages for you to make your own notes as you read through - Be ready with your highlighter and pen. Over time you'll find this book can be your go-to reference tool, especially when you start going through the purchasing process.

I've also included a glossary of the most common AI terms in the back of this book that you can refer to anytime. This extra resource will soon help you to feel confident and making informed business decisions about AI - No longer bamboozled by the technical jargon that flies around so happily in the IT world.

One caveat though, I'm definitely not an Artificial Intelligence guru - My experience is in the field of IT Business Analysis, evaluating over 100 software products for business customers. To make this book the most useful it can be, I used AI to assist me writing the technical sections. As there is controversy about AI "scraping" information from online sites without permission, I ran the AI material through an industry standard, paid plagiarism checker to provide relevant citations.

In the back section of this book you'll find a full reference list including my own research and that of the AI products I used, some of which you might find very useful to read.

And to be absolutely transparent, I'm not affiliated with any AI product, supplier or organisation, nor do I receive any payment or gifts for the products noted in this book. Any opinions in this book are my own and based on my 25 years experience as an IT Business Analyst.

That's enough preamble. Let's start your first step into becoming an *Informed Customer*... Artificial Intelligence Basics.

To your success,

Helen.

Chapter 1

AI BASICS YOU NEED TO KNOW

1. AI BASICS YOU NEED TO KNOW

In this chapter you'll get introduced to the concept of Artificial Intelligence, find out what the three major fields of AI there are and how they are often used in small business.

By this point you're probably already starting to feel a bit panicky - Worrying about the weird computer terms and other yucky stuff that you'll have to learn.

I understand.

That's why I've designed this section so we can walk (virtually) hand-in-hand through the techie stuff - very, very, s-l-o-w-l-y....

Take a long, deep breath and relax.

This is supposed to be fun!

See you inside.

WHAT IS AI?

Artificial Intelligence is a complicated beast with many layers, depending on your viewpoint. So for simplicity's sake, I've used Dent Global's definition because it fits in well with the Small Business model.

Here it is...

AI refers to the ability of machines to perform tasks that would normally require human intelligence, such as understanding language, recognising patterns and making decisions.

There are various subfields of AI, including: machine learning, natural language processing and robotics.

- DENT Global

AI BASICS YOU NEED TO KNOW

1. Machine Learning Summary

Machine learning is when computers learn to do things on their own by looking at examples and figuring out how to do them. The computers improve and make more incredibly accurate predictions based on patterns that they identify in the data.

The process of machine learning typically involves feeding large amounts of data into an algorithm or statistical model, which adjusts its parameters each time, to identify patterns and trends in the data.

As the system is fed more data, its algorithms become more refined, enabling the system to make more accurate predictions or decisions. There are three main types of machine learning: supervised learning, unsupervised learning, and reinforcement learning.

In supervised learning, the system is trained using labeled data to make predictions about new unlabeled data. In unsupervised learning, the system is trained using unlabeled data and must find patterns or relationships in the data on its own.

In reinforcement learning, the system is trained to make decisions and take actions by being rewarded or penalised based on its actions. Machine learning algorithms are used in a wide variety of applications, including recommendation engines (like Netflix's movie recommendations), predictive maintenance in manufacturing, fraud detection in banking, and image recognition in healthcare.

AI BASICS YOU NEED TO KNOW

Let's look at machine learning another way...

Once upon a time in the city of Saturna, there was a powerful force known as Machine Learning. Machine Learning was a branch of artificial intelligence that enabled computers to learn from data and improve their performance over time without being explicitly programmed.

In Saturna, machine learning played a vital role in various aspects of daily life. One day, a young woman named Mia was browsing through her favorite online bookstore. To her delight, the store's recommendation system, powered by machine learning, suggested a book that perfectly matched her interests. The system had analysed Mia's reading history and preferences, helping her discover a new favourite author.

Elsewhere in Saturna, a team of cybersecurity experts was using machine learning to protect the city's digital infrastructure.

The machine learning system could detect and analyse unusual patterns in network traffic, identifying potential cyber threats before they could cause harm. This proactive approach to cybersecurity kept Saturna's systems secure and its citizens' data safe.

The machine learning system could detect and analyse unusual patterns in network traffic, identifying potential cyber threats before they could cause harm.

This proactive approach to cybersecurity kept Saturna's systems secure and its citizens' data safe.

Meanwhile, in the heart of Saturna, a traffic management system powered by machine learning was revolutionising the city's transportation. By analysing real-time traffic data, the system could optimise traffic signals and predict congestion, reducing travel times and minimising traffic jams. The citizens of Saturna enjoyed smoother commutes and a cleaner environment, thanks to the reduced vehicle emissions.

With each passing day, the Machine Language powers grew stronger, transforming the way humans and technology interacted, making the world a better place.

AI BASICS YOU NEED TO KNOW

2. Natural Language Processing Summary

Natural Language Processing (NLP) is a type of artificial intelligence that helps computers understand human language. It's like teaching a computer to speak and understand human language just like we do!

NLP is used in many applications, such as chatbots, virtual assistants, and voice recognition software. It allows these applications to understand what we're saying and respond in a way that makes sense to us.

NLP works by breaking down human language into smaller parts, such as words and phrases, and analysing them to understand their meaning. It also takes into account the context in which the language is being used, such as the tone of voice or the situation in which the language is being spoken.

For example, if you ask a virtual assistant to play a song, NLP will analyse your request and understand that you want to listen to music. It will then search for the song you requested and play it for you.

Overall, NLP is an amazing technology that helps us communicate with computers in a more natural and intuitive way. It's like having a conversation with a friend, but your friend is a computer.

AI BASICS YOU NEED TO KNOW

Some of the most common techniques used in NLP include:

1. **Tokenisation**: Breaking down text into individual words or phrases.

2. **Part-of-speech tagging**: Identifying the grammatical structure of a sentence, such as identifying which words are nouns, verbs, adjectives, etc.

3. **Named entity recognition**: Identifying and categorising named entities in text, such as people, places, and organisations.

4. **Sentiment analysis:** Analysing the tone and emotion of text, such as determining whether a review is positive or negative.

5. **Machine translation**: Translating text from one language to another.

NLP is used in many different industries, including healthcare, finance, and marketing. For example, in healthcare, NLP can be used to analyse medical records and identify patterns that can help doctors make better diagnoses. In finance, NLP can be used to analyse news articles and social media posts to predict stock prices. In marketing, NLP can be used to analyse customer feedback and identify areas for improvement.

Overall, NLP is a powerful technology that has many different applications.

AI BASICS YOU NEED TO KNOW

Let's look at natural language processing another way...

Once upon a time in the land of Jadesville, there was a magical force called Natural Language Processing (NLP). NLP was a unique form of artificial intelligence that had the power to understand, interpret, and generate human language.

It was a bridge between the world of humans and the realm of technology, enabling them to communicate effortlessly. In Jadesville, NLP played a vital role in the lives of its inhabitants. It helped them in various ways, making their lives easier and more efficient.

One day, a businessman named Tom was preparing for an important meeting with international clients. Tom was worried about the language barrier, but NLP came to his rescue. With a real-time translation tool powered by NLP, Tom was able to communicate with his clients seamlessly, impressing them with his presentation and securing an important deal.

Elsewhere in Jadesville, a customer support center was bustling with activity. NLP-powered chatbots were assisting customers with their queries, providing quick and accurate responses. These chatbots understood the customers' concerns and offered helpful solutions, improving customer satisfaction and reducing the workload of human support agents.

The incredible powers for good of Natural Language Processing continued to weave its way into the fabric of Jadesville, transforming the way humans and technology interacted and making the world a better place.

AI BASICS YOU NEED TO KNOW

3. Robotics Summary

Robotics is a fascinating field that combines engineering, computer science, and sometimes even biology to create robots. Robots are machines that can do tasks on their own or with some guidance from humans. They can be used in many different areas, like manufacturing, healthcare, and exploring space.

The basic elements of robotics are:

1. Mechanical Design: Robots need a body, or structure, to hold all their parts together. This can include things like arms, legs, wheels, or tracks.

2. Actuators: These are the "muscles" of a robot. Actuators, like motors or pistons, help robots move their parts, like arms or wheels. They can be powered by electricity, air pressure, or liquids.

3. Sensors: Robots need to "see" and "feel" their surroundings to work well. Sensors and cameras help them do that by collecting information about things like temperature, distance, or the colour of an object.

4. Control Systems: Robots need a "brain" to make decisions and control their actions. This is usually a computer or micro-controller that processes information from sensors and sends commands to the actuators.

AI BASICS YOU NEED TO KNOW

5. Power Source: Robots need energy to work. They can get this energy from batteries, solar panels, or by plugging into a wall socket.

6. Software and Algorithms: Robots need instructions to know what to do.

7. Human-Robot Interaction: Since robots often work with or around humans, it's important to make sure they can communicate and co-operate safely.

AI BASICS YOU NEED TO KNOW

Let's look at robotics another way...

Once upon a time in the futuristic city of Mindville, there was a remarkable force known as Robotics. Robotics was the science and engineering behind designing, building, and operating robots. These robots were capable of performing various tasks, making the lives of Mindville's citizens more efficient and enjoyable. In Mindville, robots played a significant role in many aspects of daily life.

One day, a talented surgeon named Dr. Amelia was performing a delicate operation. With the assistance of a surgical robot, she was able to make precise incisions and navigate the patient's body with unparalleled accuracy. The robot's steady hands and advanced vision system allowed Dr. Amelia to perform the surgery with minimal invasiveness, leading to a faster recovery for her patient.

Elsewhere in Mindville, a team of search and rescue robots was dispatched to locate a group of hikers lost in the mountains. Equipped with advanced sensors and cameras, the robots could navigate the treacherous terrain and withstand harsh weather conditions. They found the hikers and guided them to safety, demonstrating the life-saving potential of robotics.

In the heart of Mindville, a friendly robot named Mindi served as a companion for the elderly residents of a care home. Mindi could engage in conversations, play games, and even monitor the health of the residents. The robot provided companionship and support, improving the quality of life for the seniors and giving their families peace of mind. The wide-ranging capabilities of Robotics continued to support the people of Mindville, improving their standard of living and safety.

AI BASICS YOU NEED TO KNOW

Major AI Product Types in Sales and Marketing

Refer to: *Chapter 10: Features to Look For in Sales & Marketing AI* for what to look for with each product type.

Chatbots: A conversational AI tool that can assist with customer service, sales, and engagement.

Customer Relationship Management: A software tool that helps businesses manage their interactions with customers and potential customers. It typically includes features such as contact management, sales management, marketing automation, and customer service and support.

Computer Vision: A tool that enables computers to analyse and make sense of images and videos, including object recognition, image segmentation, and motion detection. Computer vision has a wide range of applications, including self-driving cars, facial recognition, medical imaging, and more.

Cybersecurity: A tool that protects computers, servers, mobile devices, electronic systems, networks, and data from digital attacks or unauthorised access.

Email Marketing: Tools that segment, personalise, schedule and automate marketing emails.

Personalisation: Tools that segment the customer base and send personalised messages at the right time. e.g. Birthdays and other special events.

AI BASICS YOU NEED TO KNOW

Predictive Analytics: Tools that use statistical and machine learning modeling techniques to analyse data and forecast future outcomes.

Recommendation Engines: Tools that provide tailored suggestions to individual customers based on their preferences and buying behaviour.

Sentiment Analysis: Tools that analyse customer moods in real-time, including identifying irony and humour.

Social Media: Tools that enhance the customer experience on social media platforms. This broad term includes specific AI products like Chatbots, Personalisation/Recommendation Engines and Virtual Assistants.

Chatbots are definitely a lot of fun to work with, but keep your feet firmly on the ground by fact checking the results it gives you.

Protect your decision-making capability - Be sure about the information that you base those decisions on.

Chapter 2

SMALL BUSINESS USING AI

2. SMALL BUSINESS USING AI

The objective of this chapter is to give you a starting point when thinking about how you might use AI products in your own small business.

To achieve this goal I have asked AI to write some stories, each one focusing on a different type of small business - Bringing to life how different AI product types could be used improve sales and marketing performance.

The stories are not modelled on any existing or past business and the **results** presented in the stories are **not real**. They are, however, representative of what could be done in that particular scenario. They are intended for educational purposes only.

Please take the time to read each story, because different AI types are showcased throughout. Even though the small business in the story may be different to yours, the story may inspire you to investigate that particular type of AI product.

SMALL BUSINESS USING AI STORIES

1. Catering company

Sarah owns a small catering company and wants to expand into the online meal delivery business.

She uses *Amazon SageMaker* to analyse her customer data, such as dietary requirements and previous orders, to develop personalised meal plans and recommendations.

AI Product Type: *Machine Learning*
By leveraging Machine Learning, Sarah's online meal delivery business can create custom menus, improve customer satisfaction and improve sales.

2. Shoe shop

Adam runs a small business selling high-quality, personally crafted shoes. He has been collecting data of his customers' preferences and order histories over the past five years.

Adam wants to use AI to help create personalised shoe recommendations based on customer data insights. He begins using *TensorFlow*, building and training its machine learning models to analyse his business data.

AI Product Type: *Machine Learning*
By leveraging Machine Learning, Adam can make personalised product recommendations, improve his customer experience, and increase sales.

SMALL BUSINESS USING AI STORIES

3. Marketing agency

Maddie runs a small marketing agency that offers social media management services. She uses *Google Cloud Natural Language API* to gather insights from customer feedback, online reviews, and social media posts.

Maddie and her team extract insights such as customer sentiment to determine if customers feel positively or negatively about particular products and services.

AI Product Type: *Natural Language Processing, Sentiment Analysis*
The insights gathered help Maddie and her team to tailor their marketing strategies, leading to improved conversion rates.

4. Real estate agency

John runs a small real estate agency and wants to increase his lead generation rate. He uses *IBM Watson Language Translator* to translate his company's website content into different languages to reach a wider audience.

AI Product Type: *Natural Language Processing*
By translating his website content into his customers' preferred languages, John provided a better customer experience, reached more customers, improved his search engine optimisation (SEO) and improved sales.

SMALL BUSINESS USING AI STORIES

5. Curtain shop

Alex is a small business owner who runs a home décor company selling custom-made curtains. To improve his online sales, he uses *Google Cloud Vision* to analyse the images customers uploaded of their living spaces, providing instant personalised window treatment recommendations.

AI Product Type: *Computer Vision*
By implementing AI, Alex's small business can provide personalised curtain recommendations, while enhancing his brand, through the availability of 24/7 customer quotes.

6. Product packaging design

Tony runs a small business that designs and produces packaging materials. He uses *Amazon Rekognition* to analyse images of existing package designs to identify trends and potential improvements. AI provides valuable insights into customer preferences for packaging colours and images.

AI Product Type: *Computer Vision*
Using these insights, Tony can design and test his packaging solutions, to provide designs that resonate well with customers.

SMALL BUSINESS USING AI STORIES

7. Online gift store

Lily runs an online store selling handmade gifts. She uses *Microsoft Power BI* to analyse her sales data gathered over the past five years about customer purchase behaviour, browsing history, order and cart abandonment history.

AI Product Type: *Predictive Analytics*
By leveraging AI, Lily and her team can predict which products will be most popular for a particular holiday season, reducing stock waste. They can also create personalised product recommendations, leading to enhanced customer loyalty and increased sales.

8. Clothing store

Kate owns a retail store selling eco-friendly clothing. She uses *Microsoft Azure to* analyse past sales and website customer search history data to predict the next season's fashion trends.

AI Product Type: *Predictive Analytics*
By using AI, Kate's small business can order the right stock, streamline inventory and increase sales.

SMALL BUSINESS USING AI STORIES

9. IT services

Rachel is a small business owner who operates an IT services company. She integrates the *Tars* chatbot to provide friendly and helpful support to customers with technical issues.

AI Product Type: *Chatbots*
By using AI, Rachel's business can provide 24/7 customer support, which increases her customer satisfaction and loyalty. She can also use AI to send follow-up emails to customers, reminding them about ongoing services or promotions leading to increased sales.

10. Online kitchen appliances

Danny runs an online store specialising in kitchen appliances. He uses *Dialogflow* to provide responsive messaging services for his customers. The chatbot answers customers' frequently asked questions on product features, issues, and delivery schedules.

AI Product Type: *Chatbots*
By using AI, Danny has increased his customer satisfaction levels while automating routine manual tasks. Providing prompt and helpful information to his customers improved their buying experience, leading to increased sales and brand loyalty.

SMALL BUSINESS USING AI STORIES

11. Online running shoes

Michael runs an online shoe store selling running shoes. He used *UiPath* to create automated data entry tasks, such as addressing and order details that typically would have taken a few hours to complete.

AI Product Type: *Robotic Process Automation*
By automating repetitive manual tasks, Michael frees up more time to focus on developing new marketing strategies and improving sales.

12. Car rental company

James is a small business owner who operates a car rental company. He uses *UiPath* to automate data entry and document verification processes involved in managing rental bookings, from reservations to payments.

AI Product Type: *Robotic Process Automation*
By automating repetitive manual tasks, James's small business can provide an efficient service to multiple customers at the same time, resulting in increased customer satisfaction and bookings.

SMALL BUSINESS USING AI STORIES

Now, let's take a deeper look at specific business activities, using AI products

13. Small Business Marketing

As a small business owner, Elise wanted to use AI-powered marketing tools to write her marketing materials. This would save her time while creating effective and engaging content for her customers.

Elise would start by researching and selecting the best AI-powered marketing tools for her business needs and budget.

Once she has selected the right AI tools, she would input information about her business, products, and target audience, specifying the type of marketing materials she wanted to generate. This included social media posts, email newsletters, sale webpages, blog articles and product descriptions.

Using AI, Elise could generate high-quality marketing copy that was not only persuasive and engaging but also aligned with her brand voice and messaging.

Using AI, Elise would generate blog articles that are informative and engaging. The AI product *Google Bard* would use natural language processing (NLP) and machine learning algorithms to analyse her input and generate copy that would be optimised for customer engagement and sales conversion, helping her business to stand out in a crowded market.

SMALL BUSINESS USING AI STORIES

Using a *Google Cloud Natural Language API* to gather insights from customer feedback, online reviews, and social media posts would provide Elise with insights and recommendations for improving her marketing strategy, helping her to stay ahead of the competition and grow her business. Using AI-powered marketing tools would help Elise to streamline her marketing efforts and improve the effectiveness of her sales campaigns. All this while maintaining a personal touch and connection with her customers!

Overall, using AI supports Elise's goals of improving her business marketing. She would be able to generate high-quality marketing materials in a fraction of the time it would take to write them herself (although with a little editing) allowing her to focus on other aspects of her business, without sacrificing her time or resources.

AI Product Types: *Natural Language Processing, Sentiment Analysis, Social Media*

SMALL BUSINESS USING AI STORIES

14. Independent bookshop

Meet Sam, the owner of a small independent bookstore specialising in rare and hard-to-find books. Sam's business was struggling to increase sales due to his time limitations in reaching out to new customers and a having a lack of insights into their preferences.

Sam decided to leverage AI products to improve this situation. He implemented a recommendation engine, *Qloo* and the *Tars chatbot* for the bookstore's website to improve customer experience and engagement.

Using the recommendation engine, Sam was able to provide personalised book recommendations to each customer based on their past purchases and browsing history. By analysing customer histories with machine learning algorithms, the recommendation engine generated highly accurate and relevant book selections.

The chatbot enhanced his customers' experience and engagement on the bookstore's website as it was designed to offer customers support, answer frequently asked questions, and provide detailed product recommendations based on their interests.

Sam's customers greatly appreciated the personalised recommendations and found the chatbot helpful in finding the books they were looking for, leading to them returning to the site regularly and recommending Sam's bookstore to others.

SMALL BUSINESS USING AI STORIES

As a result of implementing AI tools, Sam's sales numbers increased dramatically.

Furthermore, the personalised recommendations generated helped Sam to fine-tune his bookstore's inventory, reducing the stocking of unpopular books and investing in more popular titles, ultimately leading to cost savings and increased sales.

Sam learned that by investing in AI products, his independent bookstore was able to keep up with the larger chain bookstores, providing customers with a personalised, quality service

AI Product Types: *Recommendation engine, Chatbot*

SMALL BUSINESS USING AI STORIES

15. Financial planner

Meet Brenton, the owner of a financial planning company that specialises in retirement planning and wealth management.

Brenton's business was struggling to increase sales because he didn't have the time to reach out to new customers, understanding what they really wanted.

Brenton decided to leverage AI products to improve his sales and reach to potential customers. He installed a chatbot on his company's website and integrated AI predictive analytics tools to provide much needed customer insights.

Using the chatbot, Brenton was able to offer 24/7 customer support, provide instant responses to customer queries, and assist customers with setting appointments. At the same time, the chatbot collected data about customer requirements and preferences, pre-qualifying them as potential customers.

Brenton then used the AI-powered predictive analysis product *Microsoft Azure* to analyse the new customer data, together with market trends, and transactions histories. The AI product used this information together with his customer's priorities, risks, and financial goals, giving him exactly the information he needed to create tailored financial offers for each customer.

SMALL BUSINESS USING AI STORIES

After implementing these AI products, Brenton reported an increase in sales. He learned that by leveraging the power of AI to personalise his services, not only could he free up time to generate improved financial products but he greatly increased his number of qualified customer leads.

The integration of AI technology not only improved the performance of Brenton's business but also enabled him to deliver superior services that his customers highly valued.

AI Product Types: *Chatbot, Predictive Analytics*

SMALL BUSINESS USING AI STORIES

16. Self-published author

Meet Isabel, a self-published author who wants to market her books more effectively, increasing sales. Isabel sells her books online, but she's struggling to get her books in front of the right audience.

Isabel decides to leverage AI products to promote her books more effectively and reach out to potential customers. She does this by purchasing a chatbot and *ChatGPT* to help streamline her marketing campaigns.

Isabel trains her chatbot to answer frequently asked questions about her works, title availability, and offer personalised recommendations to customers based on their site browsing or purchasing behaviour.

The chatbot collected customer data while assisting with their enquiries, providing valuable information to Isabel on their reading preferences. This helped Isabel to target potential customers with tailored marketing offers, which she used *ChatGPT* to draft.

Isabel also integrated the AI-powered analytics tool *Tableau* to analyse customer behaviour together with social trends. The data from these analytics helped Isabel identify how people engage with her books and what they love that makes them shareable. Isabel used the data insights to create even more onpoint marketing material.

SMALL BUSINESS USING AI STORIES

Isabel learned that the AI products helped her business to:

1. Increase Sales: Using *ChatGPT* to generate high quality marketing material, such as product listings, email sequences and offers described in sales landing pages, Isabel saw a significant increase in her number of books sold.

2. Improve her customer's experience: Customers appreciated the personalised recommendations and found the chatbot helpful in finding the books they were looking for, making them happy while building brand loyalty.

3. Market more efficiently: The AI products provided valuable customer insights that enabled Isabel to optimise her marketing strategy. She reduced overhead costs while streamlining her marketing campaigns.

In summary, by leveraging the power of AI, Isabel was able to streamline her marketing campaigns, optimise her sales channels and improve her business bottom line all while enhancing her customer's experience and building their loyalty.

AI Product Types: *Chatbot, Predictive Analytics, Recommendation Engine*

SMALL BUSINESS USING AI STORIES

17. High-ticket business coach

Meet Peter, a business coach who provides high-ticket coaching services for entrepreneurs. Peter knew that there was a high demand for the type of services he offered, but he faced significant challenges in marketing his business and increasing his reach to potential customers while working on his own.

He was unsure about how to target his customers and did not have the resources to spend on extensive marketing campaigns.

Peter decided to leverage AI products to market his coaching services and increase sales. He began by deploying a chatbot on his website that could answer frequently asked questions, provide customer support, and book appointments.

Peter also implemented the AI predictive analytics tool *IBM's Watson* to analyse customer preferences, interests and purchase histories to identify potential customers and provide better targeted offerings instead of using complicated forms or surveys. He used *ChatGPT* to create upgraded marketing material using the new data.

Then Peter implemented Natural Language Processing (NLP) to offer personalised services, eliminating the need to hire additional support staff. He also leveraged AI voice assistants to enable clients to access any resources they needed to be successful in their coaching journey.

SMALL BUSINESS USING AI STORIES

Peter found that the AI products helped his business to:

1. **Increase Sales**: Using *ChatGPT* to generate high quality marketing material, such as product listings, email sequences and offers described in sales landing pages, Peter saw a significant surge in the number of clients he signed up, resulting in an increase in revenue.

2. **Improve his customer's experience**: The chatbot provided 24/7 support, instant query responses and help with common issues greatly his customer's satisfaction levels.

3. **Reduced costs**: The use of AI products saved on costs associated with hiring support staff, marketing campaigns and customer acquisition, which increased business profitability.

4. **Provide personalised customer service** and support while harvesting valuable customer data and making appointment bookings.

5. **Free up valuable time** to develop insightful, personalised coaching plans.

In summary, by leveraging the power of AI, Peter was able to increase his client base in a manageable way while reducing overhead costs, desiging improved product offerings and increasing customer loyalty.

AI Product Types: *Chatbots, Natural Language Processing, Personalisation Engine, Predictive Analytics*

MY NOTES

Imagination is everything.

It is the preview of life's coming attractions.

- Albert Einstein

Chapter 3

AI ADVANTAGES FOR SMALL BUSINESS

3. AI ADVANTAGES FOR SMALL BUSINESS

Let's spend a little time looking at the range of advantages that using AI products can give a small business.

We won't go too deep here, because there are plenty of AI sales people who are shouting about their wares from the roof tops - And they have amazing websites that they can't wait to show you!

AI ADVANTAGES FOR SMALL BUSINESS

1

Improves efficiency

AI can help small businesses to analyse data faster and more accurately, which can lead to insights that help improve operational processes and reduce waste.

2

Reduces operating costs

By using AI, small businesses can reduce costs, such as customer service and data entry, marketing and copywriting, while still delivering high-quality results.

3

Increases profits

AI technology can quickly analyse data sets and draw accurate predictions, to optimise pricing strategies through the analysis of customer behaviour and market trends.

4

Improves competitive advantage

Using AI, small business can predict customer behaviour quickly, and in doing so they can adapt their products and services to meet changing market needs before their competition, who don't have the advantage of AI support.

5

Increases productivity

With AI, small business can automate time-consuming manual processes such as inventory management and quality control, improving accuracy, reducing errors and freeing up team members for higher-level tasks.

AI ADVANTAGES FOR SMALL BUSINESS

6

Create better customer experiences

AI can help small businesses personalise their marketing efforts by analysing customer data and creating targeted campaigns that are more likely to resonate with individual customers.

7

Predictive analytics

AI can analyse large amounts of data to identify patterns and predict future outcomes, such as which customers are most likely to churn or which products are likely to sell well, enabling marketers to make more informed decisions.

8

Provides insights into customer behaviour

AI provides insights into customer behaviour by analysing data such as purchasing history, interests, and social media activity, helping small businesses understand their customers better and make more informed decisions.

9

Improves market message targeting

AI provides targeted marketing messaging by analysing customer data and preferences, allowing small businesses to tailor marketing messages that resonate with their audience and increase the chances of conversion.

10

Supports better decision making

AI can generate ideas based on data insights, identifying trends and patterns, and offering suggestions that can lead to new business opportunities.

AI ADVANTAGES FOR SMALL BUSINESS

11

Reduce risk

AI can help identify and protect against potential risks, such as fraud and cyber security threats.

12

Banishes the "blank page" problem

AI can provide a list of ideas for possible social media posts, advertising blurb, presentation or webinar content, removing the fear of starting your project with a blank page.

13

Improved customer service

AI-powered chatbots can help small businesses provide 24/7 customer service, answering common questions and resolving issues quickly and efficiently across any time zone.

14

Faster lead generation

AI can help small businesses identify and target high-quality leads, increasing the chances of converting them into paying customers.

15

Improved Sales Forecasting

AI can help small businesses forecast sales more accurately, allowing them to make better decisions about inventory management and resource allocation.

MY NOTES

Chapter 4

COMMON CONCERNS SMALL BUSINESS HAVE ABOUT AI

4. COMMON CONCERNS SMALL BUSINESS HAVE ABOUT AI

In this chapter we'll take a look at the five most common concerns that Small Business have about AI.

Understanding the issues around this technology helps you to be better prepared, to make more informed decisions and feel comfortable when you talk to AI suppliers about their products.

AI is new to everyone. To help you more, I've included some strategies that you can consider to address each concern.

COMMON CONCERNS SMALL BUSINESS HAVE ABOUT AI

1. Monetary investment

Implementing AI technology can be expensive and require a significant financial investment.

Suggested Strategies

1. Exploring open-source AI solutions and platforms that are cost-effective and suitable for small businesses.

These platforms often provide a wide range of tools and resources that can help small business owners implement AI technology without breaking the bank.

Popular open-source AI platforms include:

- TensorFlow (natural language processing, image recognition).
- Scikit-Learn (data analysis and modelling).
- Apache MXNet (deep learning library).
- H20.ai (wide range of machine learning algorithms and tools).
- RapidMiner (data science platform).

2. Use free or cheaper products such as ChatGPT for marketing, copywriting and document writing services.

3. Consider partnering with AI consulting firms or freelancers who specialise in implementing AI solutions for small businesses, as they can provide tailored guidance and support at a more affordable cost.

COMMON CONCERNS SMALL BUSINESS HAVE ABOUT AI

2. Security and privacy

As AI systems become more sophisticated, they become easier targets for hackers and cybercriminals. AI systems can also be used to collect and store personal data without user consent.

Suggested Strategies

1. **Use Secure AI Frameworks and Libraries**: Choose AI frameworks and libraries that prioritise security and have a strong community support. This ensures that any security vulnerabilities are quickly identified and fixed. Some popular secure AI frameworks include TensorFlow, PyTorch, and Scikit-Learn.

2. **Data Encryption**: Encrypt sensitive data both at rest and in transit to protect it from unauthorised access. Use strong encryption algorithms and key management practices to ensure the security of your data.

3. **Access Control**: Implement strict access control policies to limit who can access your AI systems and data. This includes using strong authentication methods, such as multi-factor authentication, and implementing role-based access control to ensure that users only have access to the data and systems they need.

4. Regular Security Audits: Conduct regular security audits to identify potential vulnerabilities in your AI systems and infrastructure. This includes penetration testing, vulnerability scanning, and code reviews to ensure that your systems are secure and up-to-date.

5. Employee Training: Educate your team about the importance of data security and the potential risks associated with AI systems. Provide regular training on best practices for securing AI systems and handling sensitive data.

6. Privacy-by-Design: Implement privacy-by-design principles when developing AI systems. This means considering privacy and data protection from the initial stages of system design and ensuring that personal data is only collected and stored when necessary and with user consent.

7. Monitor and Update: Continuously monitor your AI systems for any unusual activity or potential security threats. Keep your systems updated with the latest security patches and updates to protect against known vulnerabilities.

8. Backup and Disaster Recovery: Regularly backup your data and have a disaster recovery plan in place to ensure business continuity in case of a security breach or system failure.

COMMON CONCERNS SMALL BUSINESS HAVE ABOUT AI

3. Job losses

AI technology can automate certain jobs and tasks, leading to job losses and a decrease in economic opportunity.

Suggested Strategies

1. **Reskilling and Upskilling**: Invest in employee training programs to help them acquire new skills and adapt to the changing job market. This can include training in data analysis, programming, or other areas relevant to the business and the AI technology being implemented.

2. **Job Redesign**: Instead of completely replacing jobs with AI, redesign job roles to complement the technology. This can involve assigning employees to higher-value tasks that require human creativity, empathy, and decision-making, while AI handles repetitive and mundane tasks.

3. **Encourage Entrepreneurship**: Support and encourage employees to explore entrepreneurial opportunities within the company or in the broader market. This can lead to the creation of new businesses and job opportunities.

4. **Collaboration between AI and Humans**: Promote a collaborative work environment where AI systems and human employees work together to achieve better results. This can lead to increased productivity and innovation, creating new job opportunities in the long run.

COMMON CONCERNS SMALL BUSINESS HAVE ABOUT AI

5. Focus on Human-Centric Services: Small businesses can differentiate themselves by offering personalised, human-centric services that AI technology cannot replicate. This can help maintain and even create new job opportunities in areas where human interaction is highly valued.

6. Community Engagement: Engage with local communities and educational institutions to promote awareness of the changing job market and the skills required for future jobs. This can help prepare the workforce for the impact of AI technology on employment.

7. Government and Industry Collaboration: Advocate for government policies and industry initiatives that support workforce development, job creation, and social safety nets for those affected by AI-driven job displacement.

8. Ethical AI Implementation: Adopt ethical guidelines for AI implementation in your small business, ensuring that the technology is used responsibly and with consideration for its impact on employees and the broader community.

COMMON CONCERNS SMALL BUSINESS HAVE ABOUT AI

4. Biased output

AI algorithms can easily be biased due to the data sets used to train them. This can lead to inaccurate results and decisions, which can be both costly and unethical.

Suggested Strategies

1. Diverse and Representative Data: Ensure that the data sets used to train AI algorithms are diverse and representative of the target population. This helps to minimise bias and improve the accuracy of the AI system's predictions and decisions.

2. Data Preprocessing: Clean and preprocess the data before using it to train AI algorithms. This includes handling missing values, removing outliers, and balancing class distributions to reduce the impact of bias in the data.

3. Bias Detection and Mitigation Techniques: Implement bias detection and mitigation techniques during the AI model development process. This can include re-sampling techniques, re-weighting instances, or using fairness-aware machine learning algorithms that are designed to minimise bias.

4. Regular Model Evaluation: Continuously evaluate the performance of AI algorithms on diverse and representative test data sets. Monitor for any signs of bias and update the models accordingly to ensure fairness and accuracy.

COMMON CONCERNS SMALL BUSINESS HAVE ABOUT AI

5. **Transparency and Explainability**: Adopt AI models that are transparent and explainable, allowing stakeholders to understand the decision-making process and identify potential bias.

6. **Ethical AI Guidelines**: Develop and follow ethical AI guidelines for your small business, ensuring that AI systems are designed and implemented with fairness, accountability, and transparency in mind.

7. **Employee Training**: Train employees on the potential bias in AI algorithms and the importance of using diverse and representative data sets. Encourage a culture of ethical AI development and use within the organisation.

8. **External Audits**: Consider engaging external experts or third-party organisations to audit your AI systems for potential bias and provide recommendations for improvement.

9. **Collaboration with Diverse Teams**: Involve diverse teams in the AI development process, including people from different backgrounds, genders, and ethnicities. This can help to identify and address potential bias in AI algorithms.

10. **Continuous Improvement**: Treat AI systems as an ongoing process of learning and improvement. Regularly update and refine AI models to minimise bias and ensure that they continue to provide accurate and fair results.

COMMON CONCERNS SMALL BUSINESS HAVE ABOUT AI

5. Data requirements

AI applications need significant amounts of data to work effectively. If the right data is not available, AI applications may struggle to generate the desired results.

Suggested Strategies

1. **Data Augmentation**: Enhance your existing data by applying various techniques such as rotation, scaling, or flipping to create new data points. This can help improve the performance of AI applications even with limited data.

2. **Transfer Learning**: Utilise pre-trained AI models that have been trained on large datasets and fine-tune them for your specific use. This can help overcome the limitations of having a small dataset.

3. **Synthetic Data Generation**: Create synthetic data that mimics the characteristics of your real data. This can be done using various techniques such as data simulation, generative adversarial networks (GANs), or data anonymisation.

4. **Data Partnerships**: Collaborate with other businesses or organisations to share or pool data resources, ensuring that all parties maintain data privacy and comply with relevant regulations.

5. **Open Data Sources**: Explore open data sources available online, such as government datasets or public repositories, to supplement your existing data.

COMMON CONCERNS SMALL BUSINESS HAVE ABOUT AI

Let's look at small business concerns about AI another way...

Once upon a time in a small village, there was a woman named Sarah who owned a small business selling handmade crafts. Despite her hard work, Sarah struggled to attract customers and grow her business. She was afraid to use Artificial Intelligence for sales and marketing campaigns because she didn't understand what was involved.

One day, a tech-savvy friend suggested Sarah try using AI to improve her marketing efforts. Although hesitant, Sarah decided to give it a try when her friend offered to help her through the process.

With the help of AI, Sarah was able to analyse her customer data, create personalised marketing campaigns, and improve her online presence. As a result, her sales began to increase, and her business started to thrive.

Over time, Sarah realised that her fear of using AI was unfounded because it had actually helped her grow her business. She became more confident and open to trying new ideas and technologies.

With her newfound success, Sarah was able to expand her business and employ more people, bringing joy and prosperity to her community.

MY NOTES

Chapter 5

LESSONS I'VE LEARNED WORKING WITH AI

Tell me and I forget,

Teach me and I may remember,

Involve me and I learn.

- Benjamin Franklin

5. LESSONS I'VE LEARNED WORKING WITH AI

Over the past five years I've been interested in and learning about Artificial Intelligence products.

The public release of *ChatGPT* in late 2022 dialed up my urge to better understand what the *new kids on the block* were like and what impact they were going to have on business and society.

This chapter is a selection of the things that I've learned through trialing chatbots and creative assistants for sales and marketing. Some of them may surprise you, even make you laugh, but some are deadly serious.

I see this brave new world being akin to the movie *Jurassic Park - The Lost World.* To quote Geoff Goldblum's character, Dr Ian Malcolm -

"*Oh yeah. Oooh, ahhh, that's how it always starts.
Then later there's running and screaming.*"

Well we certainly don't want AI to go in the same direction as Dr Malcolm describes. *Being informed customers* is one of the major safeguards to coralling this wonderous technology for the benefit of business and society.

LESSONS I'VE LEARNED WORKING WITH AI

1. Use clear, unambiguous instructions when asking GPT (Generative Pre-trained Transformer) AI models, like *ChatGPT*, for information.

Use direct prompts like:

- List 10 things...
- Explain this concept...
- Create a...

2. Structure requests for information in logical groupings, that the AI model can easily digest. It can be easy to confuse AI, causing an incorrect result.

Request format:

OUTCOME + NUMBER + OBJECT + ACTION

EXAMPLE:

List [OUTCOME] *10 things* [NUMBER] *a coach needs to know* [OBJECT], to increase their marketing reach [ACTION].

3. Keep up to date with the developments in AI - especially those affecting small business. Areas of current concern are:

- IP / Copyright
- Fraud / Scams
- Data breaches
- Privacy
- Plagiarism

LESSONS I'VE LEARNED WORKING WITH AI

4. Find out where your data will be stored when using a particular AI product. Also ask the AI supplier - *Is your data covered by a Non-Disclosure Agreement?* Can the AI supplier use the data for their other customers?

Being super diligent with this, could mean the difference between your success or failure as a small business.

5. Be aware of the information you're feeding into any AI product. AI is learning from your input and may use what it's learnt to assist other customers/competitors.

Before entering information to an AI request, check to see if it contains:

- Your business strategy.
- Any commercial-in-confidence material.
- Any software development documentation, including software code.
- Anything that you wouldn't want available on the Internet, or publicly available to competitors.

LESSONS I'VE LEARNED WORKING WITH AI

6. GPT AI products are an excellent brainstorming tool, especially for creating sales and marketing artefacts.

Ask for any of these formats:

- Long sales page.
- Product description.
- Using PAS, AIDA, ACCA, BAB, CC, FAB, FE, PPF, PASTOR, PPPP, or SPIN formats for marketing.
- Social media content.
- Video content.
- Course outlines.
- And the list goes on... Be imaginative, you'll be surprised by the results you get.

I've found that it's good to ask AI for 3 or 4 variations of a creative document. I save them all to one Microsoft Word document, print that out and then use the drafts as inspiration for the final copy. It's such a time saver!

LESSONS I'VE LEARNED WORKING WITH AI

7. Changing the tone of any written artefact is super easy with AI.

Try requesting a sales advertisement be created using different tones such as:

- A persuasive tone.
- A friendly and witty tone.
- A serious, professional tone.
- A casual, yet urgent tone.
- An environmentally conscious tone.
- A warm and friendly manner.
- An emotional tone.
- In simple language at a Grade 6 level.

If the result is a little heavy on warmth, for example, ask AI to rewrite it with a little less warmth. It's up to you as to how much emphasis any tone has in your results.

Also, if you want the result to include a specific word, such as *product* instead of *tool*, include that in your instruction because the AI product refers to your instructions to construct its response.

LESSONS I'VE LEARNED WORKING WITH AI

8. Some AI products remember your last command. This is very useful when building a complex query, or the word limit per question/answer is short. ChatGPT has a *Regenerate response* button, saving even more time. Currently it looks like this:

To prompt the remainder of a complex answer to display, after receiving the first part, I've used the prompts:

- Continue
- Complete
- More
- Finish

Some prompts worked better than others, it all depended on the AI product I was using.

9. AI data isn't always real-time. When buying AI products ask the supplier how old the data was that the product was trained on. Sometimes there can be a 12 month lag. Factor that into your business requirements.

For sales and marketing purposes, it shouldn't be a big issue, but if you're asking about the prediction of market trends, it could be a problem.

LESSONS I'VE LEARNED WORKING WITH AI

10. Sometimes it's easy to forget that your AI product is a machine, just like your car or your mobile phone.
In just a few short sentences you can start thinking that the AI product has feelings. Thinking like that can skew your interpretation of its answers.

Generally, AI makes no value judgements (except for any built-in bias) and so is essentially guileless. Anything it tells you is supposed to be a fact. Treat it as such, but don't forget to do any required fact-checking.

11. Each AI tool has its own parameters, such as a word or character count for a query and a response. Some have a memory function and others don't so they need to have requests entered afresh each time. Spending time working out what the rules are initially with the AI product you decide to use, will reduce your errors and improve the AI's performance.

12. Check each response from AI. Treat AI content like a new graduate's first draft, that while is full of great material, still needs reviewing for facts and style.

13. Watch the AI Supplier costings. At the moment the price of accessing AI products seems to be wildly fluctuating. The only dependable trend is that the prices will rise. Using the AI Product Factor Rating template in this book will help you make an informed decision about getting all the functionality you need, at an affordable price.

LESSONS I'VE LEARNED WORKING WITH AI

14. If you use multiple AI products, as I have in my trials, the variation in responses should be watched for. Going forward, it's probably easier to choose an AI product that resonates with you. There are enough products on the market that you can afford to shop around to find the right fit.

15. The key thing I learned is that I, as the human, had to supply context, and often quite a lot, to get a meaningful response from AI. I quickly found that I had to be clear in my own mind, and then as the AI's instructor, to get my desired result. So planning ahead for each AI session greatly improved my productivity.

MY NOTES

Plans are worthless -

But planning is everything.

- Winston Churchill

Chapter 6

HOW A CHATBOT CAN SUPERCHARGE YOUR BUSINESS

6. HOW A CHATBOT CAN SUPERCHARGE YOUR BUSINESS

Chatbots and Creative Assistants, like *ChatGPT*, *Jasper* and *Bing ChatGPT* are the talk of the town.

Chatbots are AI-powered products that can simulate human conversations and can be integrated with various messaging platforms and internet home pages. They can also be used to generate marketing and sales material.

Let's take a look at how a chatbot could supercharge your business.

HOW A CHATBOT CAN SUPERCHARGE YOUR BUSINESS

Chatbots can boost your business performance through:

1. **Enhanced Customer Support**: A chatbot can provide instant customer support, answering frequently asked questions, providing product information, and assisting with basic troubleshooting. This improves customer satisfaction and reduces the workload on your support team.

2. **Lead Generation and Qualification**: Chatbots can engage website visitors, collect contact information, and qualify leads by asking relevant questions. This helps businesses identify potential customers and prioritise follow-up actions, ultimately boosting conversion rates and sales.

3. **Personalised Recommendations**: By analysing user preferences and behaviour, chatbots can offer personalised product recommendations and suggestions. This level of customisation enhances the customer experience, increases engagement, and drives sales by showcasing relevant products or services.

4. **Streamlined Sales Process**: Chatbots can guide customers through the sales process, providing information, answering questions, and even facilitating transactions. This automation saves time for both customers and businesses, leading to faster conversions and increased revenue.

5. **Data Collection and Analysis**: Chatbots can gather valuable data about customer interactions, preferences, and pain points. This data can be analysed to gain insights into customer behaviour, improve marketing strategies, and refine product offerings.

HOW A CHATBOT CAN SUPERCHARGE YOUR BUSINESS

6. Increased Efficiency: Chatbots can automate repetitive tasks and processes, such as appointment scheduling, order tracking, and FAQs. By handling these tasks, chatbots free up time for your team to focus on more complex and value-added activities, improving overall operational efficiency.

7. Improved User Engagement: Chatbots can engage users in interactive and conversational experiences, making interactions with your business more enjoyable and memorable. They can be customised to reflect your brand and tone of voice. This increased engagement can lead to higher customer retention, brand loyalty, and word-of-mouth referrals.

8. Cost Savings: Implementing a chatbot can be a cost-effective solution compared to hiring additional staff for customer support or sales. Chatbots can handle multiple conversations simultaneously, reducing the need for additional human resources and lowering operational costs.

9. 24/7 Availability: Unlike human agents, chatbots can provide support and assistance around-the-clock, ensuring that customers can access information and assistance whenever they need it. This availability improves customer satisfaction and helps capture potential sales opportunities outside of regular business hours.

10. Scalability: As your business grows, chatbots can easily scale to handle increased customer inquiries and interactions. They can handle a high volume of conversations without compromising response times or customer experience, ensuring that your business can handle growth without overwhelming your team.

MY NOTES

In the end,

it is important to remember

that we cannot become

what we need to be

by remaining what we are.

-Max De Pree

Chapter 7

THE 5-STEP BUSINESS AI BOOSTER PROCESS

7. THE 5-STEP BUSINESS AI BOOSTER PROCESS

In this chapter we'll walk through the exact process to follow to choose the right AI product for your small business.

Because there are so many AI products out there, it is critical that you are as informed as you can be, about your own business. AI suppliers will promise you "the world", but you may need a smaller solution, one which is tailor-made to your particular business.

Read through all the steps first, to get a broad understanding of the process and then work from *Step 1: Identify current processes*, through to *Step 5: Purchase your AI product* in order. Following these steps in order will make sure that you don't miss out any critical activities, that make you a super-informed buyer!

By the end of this process you will be the proud owner of more business intelligence than you have only dreamt about having - giving you a huge competitive advantage against your competitors, who haven't done the work needed to understand their business capabilities as well as you do now.

It always seems impossible,
until it's done.

- Nelson Mandela

THE 5-STEP BUSINESS AI BOOSTER PROCESS

The *5-Step Business AI Booster Process* has been designed to help small business owners prepare for AI technology, and on achieving that, that they can confidently carry out a rigorous evaluation process of the AI products on the market.

Using this standardised process is a critical part of the informed AI customer's toolkit. Purchase decisions become much easier to make if each step is followed before going out to market. By the end of the process, with all the action items completed, you will know more about how your business functions. You'll be able to pinpoint exactly what's needed to supercharge your small business using AI products, in a much more agile way than your toughest competitors.

In a nutshell, the five process steps are:

1. **Identify** current business processes and tasks.

2. **Evaluate** the efficiency of existing business processes.

3. **Prioritise** business processes and related tasks for AI improvement.

4. **Select** the first business process and tasks for AI automation.

5. **Purchase** your AI product, implement and measure performance.

Now let's take a look at each step in more detail.

THE 5-STEP BUSINESS AI BOOSTER PROCESS

This diagram shows that the *5-Step Business AI Booster Process* is a continuous loop. I recommend that you restart at *Step 1: Identify current processes*, as your learnings from the earlier cycles will most definitely alter your ideas and expectations about AI products.

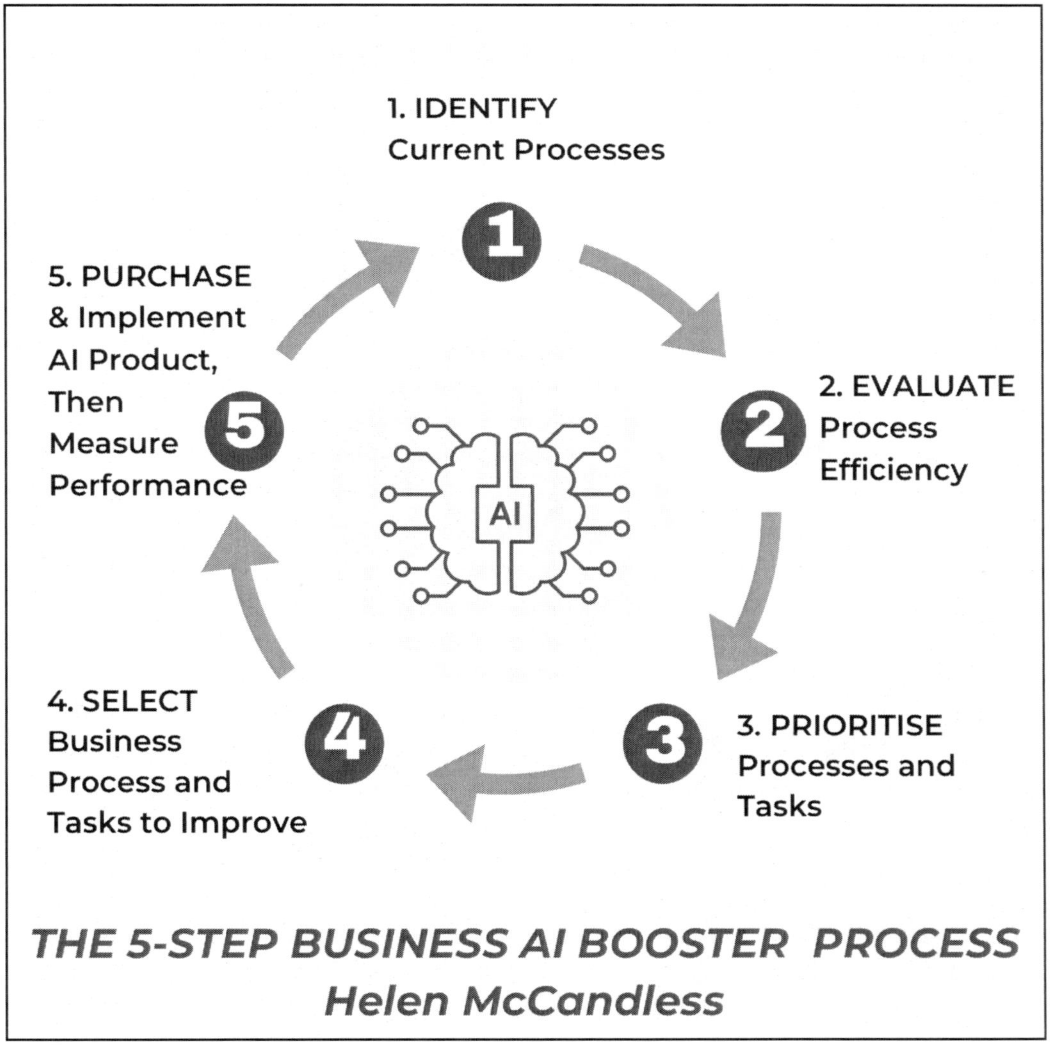

THE 5-STEP BUSINESS AI BOOSTER PROCESS

STEP 1. Identify Current Business Processes

The first step to use AI in your business is to understand the processes that your business already has in place.

As a small business, it's important to know which tasks are carried out, how often, who does them and what resources are needed to complete them.

Having a reasonable idea of how much one full cycle of a particular process costs your business is crucial to measuring the return on your investment on an AI product you purchased to automate it.

Techopedia defines a "Business Process" as:

A wide range of structured, often chained, activities or tasks conducted by people or equipment to produce a specific service or product for a particular user or consumer. Business processes are implemented to accomplish a predetermined organisational goal. Business processes occur at all organisational levels; some are visible to customers, while others are not.

An example of this is:

Process: Marketing

Tasks: Writing product descriptions, copywriting, designing advertisements, web landing page content and creating marketing images.

THE 5-STEP BUSINESS AI BOOSTER PROCESS

Here's a list of some of the more common small business processes:

- Accounting
- Advertising
- Analytics and Reporting
- Appointment scheduling
- Bookkeeping
- Customer Communications (Emails, Telephone, Web)
- Data entry
- Inventory management
- Marketing
- Orders and deliveries
- Payroll processing
- Product creation
- Recordkeeping
- Sales tracking
- Stocktaking

THE 5-STEP BUSINESS AI BOOSTER PROCESS

ACTIVITY

Write down the details of all your business processes. Use the ***Business Process Audit*** template on the next page to assist you.

Use a separate page for each process.

Then, use the template to detail the tasks involved within each process. It might help you to collaborate with your team to document an entire business process and capture every task that's involved.

Sometimes tasks are carried out using muscle-memory - there may be a step that is repeated in every task, but when asked to describe the overall process, that step is completely forgotten.

To avoid this, try watching the person carry out a process, recording everything that they do. Match up the findings with your documented business procedures (if you have some). I've seen critical steps forgotten because the action is repeated so many times a day.

To help make this mini "time and motion" study less threatening, perhaps turn it into a game, where both the staff members involved are the investigating detectives. Remember the goal is information gathering, not recrimination.

Fill out as many template sheets as you need to, until all your business processes and their tasks are documented.

BUSINESS PROCESS AUDIT

BUSINESS PROCESS: ______________________________

DATE: ______________ COST: ______________________

TASK NAME	BRIEF DESCRIPTION	FREQUENCY	RESPONSIBLE

THE 5-STEP BUSINESS AI BOOSTER PROCESS

STEP 2. Evaluate the efficiency of existing business processes

When you have completed your business process audit, it's important to drill down to the task level, to find the existing issues or problems.

List each task on the ***Business Process Task Summary*** template on the next page. Note each business process that the task relates to in the second column and record if there are any problems with the task for that business process in the third column. One task may be part of a number of business processes.

For example, there might be "clunkiness", bottlenecks, or rework happening - perhaps a customer fills out an online form but a team member has to re-key the details into the Customer Relationship Management system. Perhaps your order fulfillment process is being held up because there's only one person to take the order, update the computer record, pack and send the purchased product to the customer. Make a note of this type of problems. These could be good candidates for improvement by AI.

Fill out as many template sheets as you need to, until all tasks and the business processes they belong to are documented. The data recorded on these sheets highlights exactly where your business process problems and commonalities are. You can now use them as targets for your business AI strategy.

Now give yourself a pat on the back because today you've significantly improved your competitive advantage by intimately understanding your business.

BUSINESS PROCESS TASK SUMMARY

DATE: ____________________

TASK NAME	BUSINESS PROCESSES RELATED TO	PROBLEM? Y/N	PROBLEM DESCRIPTION

THE 5-STEP BUSINESS AI BOOSTER PROCESS

STEP 3. Prioritise your business processes and tasks

This is the step where you think critically about each task to decide whether it needs to be changed or improved, or even if the task should be done at all.

The desired result is that you will be able to clearly see which of your business processes and tasks are the most important to your business performance and consequently your bottom line and profit margins.

You'll need your completed ***Business Process Audits*** and ***Business Process Task Summaries*** to do this exercise.

Use the ***Business Process Priority Quadrant*** template on the next page. Complete a separate page for each of your business processes. For each business process, place it's tasks in one of the four quadrants.

In the template, the quadrants are divided into four levels of importance:

- High Priority
- Quite Important
- Important
- Are These Tasks Necessary?

As you may have a large number of business processes, trial using a large sized piece of paper or a white board to record the results of your research. This is a crucial step in your journey to become an informed AI customer, so give yourself and your team enough time to complete the exercise.

BUSINESS PROCESS PRIORITY QUADRANT

BUSINESS PROCESS: ________________________________

DATE: ______________

METHOD: Choose a category for each task of the business process for this page. Write the name of the task in the relevant quadrant.

HIGH PRIORITY	QUITE IMPORTANT
IMPORTANT	ARE THESE TASKS NECESSARY?

THE 5-STEP BUSINESS AI BOOSTER PROCESS

STEP 4. Select the first business process for AI

Congratulations for finishing the first three steps. I know it's been a big effort, but you're about to discover exactly which of your business processes and their associated tasks would benefit from AI improvement. Plus identify a few rogue processes that could use some pruning!

You'll need your completed ***Business Process Task Summaries*** and ***Business Process Priority Quadrants*** to do this exercise.

Use the ***High Priority Business Tasks With Issues*** template on the next page.

List each task from the High Priority Quadrant from Step 3, which have problems that you identified in Step 2. For each task, write in the business process/es they're related to and a short description about the problem. Your problem description will be what you'll use to evaluate AI products, so it's worth adding as much information as possible in this column.

When you have completed this, you'll have enough information to quickly work out which business processes and their related tasks are the most important to your business performance to improve through the use of AI.

HIGH PRIORITY BUSINESS TASKS WITH ISSUES

BUSINESS PROCESS: ______________________________

DATE: ________________________

METHOD: List each task from the High Priority Quadrants which have problems (Identified in Step 2).

TASK NAME	BUSINESS PROCESSES RELATED TO	PROBLEM DESCRIPTION

THE 5-STEP BUSINESS AI BOOSTER PROCESS

STEP 5. Select your AI product, implement and measure

Now the *rubber hits the road*, as the old saying goes.

Take some time to review what you've learned so far. Do you feel confident thinking about which AI products would best suit your needs? It's OK if you don't just yet - Be assured that you know significantly more than you did when you started reading this book. Try not to stress and remember that taking baby steps is the key to long-term success.

To refresh your memory, before moving forward, there's a quick overview of AI product types on Page 17. Perhaps read through the ***Chapter 2: Small Business Using AI*** again, to give you some more ideas about which AI products might be good for your situation.

I've included the following documents to help you with this step:

- ***AI Product Evaluation Sheet*** template. Page 92
- ***5-Step Business AI Booster Process*** checklist. Page 93
- ***Chapter 8: Factors To Consider*** Page 95
- ***Final Checklist - Before You Buy AI*** Page 111
- ***Chapter 12: Measuring Your AI Investment***. Page 159
  Mostly used after you've installed the AI product.

Call a few suppliers and talk through your needs with them. They can help you more if you clearly and simply explain the business problems you have and the outcomes you hope to achieve.

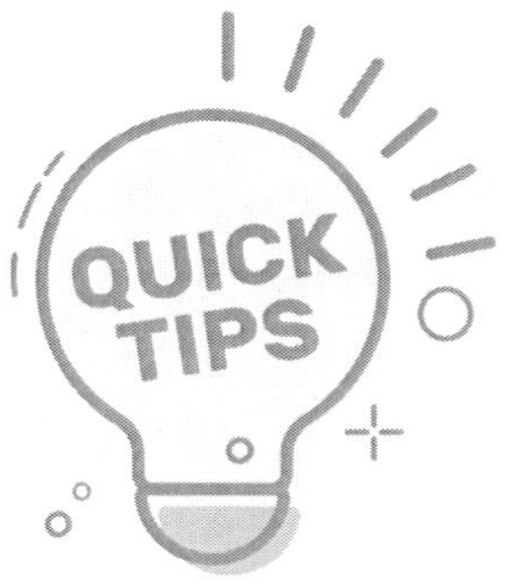

It is helpful to have a written "Use Case" - a story about your business process and tasks, explaining exactly how the business process should work and who the people "Actors" are in the story.

Don't be afraid to create a wish list of features that you'd love the AI product to have. Not all of them may be available straight away, but with the current speed of AI development, they may ready very soon.

Be open to the idea of doing a pilot project (or a trial) so you can quickly see if the AI solution is a good fit for your business.

The AI supplier may be keen to use your business as a Customer Case Study, in return for a reduced fee. If doing this interests you, ask about the possibility in your initial discussions with them.

AI PRODUCT EVALUATION SHEET

COMPANY		PRODUCT NAME	
CONTACT NAME		VERSION NUMBER	
CONTACT DETAILS		STAFF ATTENDING	
MEETING LOCATION			

EVALUATION ITEM	RATING 0-10 0=UNSATISFACTORY 10=EXCELLENT	NOTES
COST		
SECURITY		
PRIVACY		
SCALEABILITY		
INTEGRATION WITH EXISTING SYSTEMS		
BIAS/ACCURACY		
FUNCTIONALITY		
TECHNOLOGY ROADMAP		
SUPPORT		
TRAINING		
DOCUMENTATION		
PROBLEM NAME #1		
PROBLEM NAME #2		
PROBLEM NAME #3		
PROBLEM NAME #4		

THE 5-STEP BUSINESS AI BOOSTER PROCESS

CHECKLIST

Before you pick up the phone, or touch the keyboard to email an AI supplier, first check you've done these things...

1. Have you documented all your business processes and tasks, as explained on Page 82?

2. Have you reviewed all your business processes and tasks and identified any problems, as explained on Page 84?

3. Have you prioritised your business processes and tasks against their importance to your business performance, as explained on Page 86?

4. Have you identified the first process/es and related tasks that you think could be improved through AI, as explained on Page 88?

5. Have you read the additional resources provided in this book before discussing your business needs with AI suppliers, as listed on Page 90?

MY NOTES

Chapter 8

FACTORS TO CONSIDER

8. FACTORS TO CONSIDER

In this chapter we'll take a look at some major factors to consider before you purchase an AI product.

These are common issues that affect every business, so thinking about them now gives you an advantage over your competitors who may not have taken the time to be so prepared.

FACTORS TO CONSIDER

The Informed Customer

By this stage of the book, you've worked out which of your processes would be the best to start improving with AI.

You've thought about which type of sales and marketing AI product (see Page 17) might best suit your business and even had some preliminary chats with AI suppliers.

Now you can start to look more critically at the range of AI products on the market. To do this effectively, carefully consider each of the evaluation factors which I talk about in this chapter and rate them against each product using the ***AI Product Evaluation Sheet*** template on Page 92.

You will only need to check out two or three AI products to quickly see that there are significant similarities and differences. Your job is to decide which product capabilities are deal breakers for your business, or which you can live with. As with all technology, no specific product will be exactly perfect for your needs, but it does have to be "good enough".

As a rough guide, an 80/20 fit should work here. As long as you get 80% of the functionality that you need from an AI product, and that includes ALL your mandatory requirements (reporting, compliance, legislation, etc), you should be able to workaround the remaining 20%.

FACTORS TO CONSIDER

1. Ongoing budget for AI

The overall cost of AI involves multiple layers, not just the initial purchase price. Here's some to consider:

- **Initial purchase price**: Is this a once-only payment, or an annual subscription? Which level of product service suits you better? Be aware that the standard price is often light on functionality. Paying for the professional product may be cheaper in the long run.

- **Implementation timeline and cost**: Upgrading processes, training staff, adapting current technology, web pages, etc, to include the AI interface. Expected dates to deliver specific functions.

- **Reputation cost**: Is your customer-base pro or anti-AI? You might consider creating a change management plan, to ease your customers into the benefits of the new technology, or start thinking of alternate technologies if you think they need to know you're using AI.

- **Affordability**: Check that the ongoing cost of maintaining the AI product is affordable and provides a good Return on Investment. We'll look at ROI from AI products later in this guide.

FACTORS TO CONSIDER

2. User friendliness

Ease of use is a fundamental factor to implementation success.

- If the AI product is clunky, or drives unintended manual workarounds, staff and customer uptake will be problematic.
- Check that the human-to-AI product interaction is simple and smooth. Does the product use natural language processing or does it use computer code only? Do you have the expertise on your team to work with the product without too steep a learning curve? Ask about ongoing training costs to keep up to date with new developments.
- If you're considering a chatbot for customer service, check that the language it uses is appropriate for your customer base. Ask the supplier about inbuilt bias and what they've done to correct that.

3. Scalability

Scalability is just another word to describe the ability to grow, usually together with the number of customers or markets that your business has.

Can the AI product grow with your business, especially regarding the volume of requests it can process at the same time and the amount of data it can store? If not, perhaps opt for a slightly larger product capacity, which your business can grow into.

FACTORS TO CONSIDER

4. Customer support

The AI supplier should always provide a level of training and support for their products.

- Check if their "Help Desk" is local to you, as in the same country, or overseas. If so, do they provide support 24/7, or only during their own particular work hours? It can get very frustrating to deal with customer support who are asleep when you are at work, having to send emails and wait 12 hours for a response.

- Are there documented User Guides to help you work out basic problems on your own? What training is available? Better still, is there a User Group in your location, which you can join to discuss common learnings and issues?

- What level of support does the supplier offer? They may have different payment plans. In the beginning you may feel more comfortable with extra support, which can be reduced when you and your team get used to the system. This is another cost to factor into your budget calculations.

FACTORS TO CONSIDER

5. Features

From your process auditing (Page 80), you should have a clear understanding of the AI features you need.

- Check that the AI product provides those features. It may take a little lateral thinking on your part, because often automated software does have a capability, but it doesn't do it exactly the way you may have always done it.

- This is where having some process scenarios (User Stories) to show the AI supplier will come in very handy. Ask the supplier to reproduce your required outcomes with their product.

- Be aware that changing your business processes is almost certainly something that you're going to need to do. And it's probably a good time to revisit them anyway, to bring them up to date.

- If the product doesn't have a certain feature, ask the AI Supplier if it is on their *technology roadmap* - That's their technology development plan for the next 2-5 years. What you want may be planned for delivery soon. If it's not a deal breaker for you, then you may decide it's worth waiting for, or perhaps you could check out a different AI product and see what features that already has.

FACTORS TO CONSIDER

6. Integration

Find out very early from the AI supplier if their product can integrate easily with the existing technology tools in your small business.

- If the supplier tells you that you'll need to buy a whole suite of different software that "links" the AI product to your existing software, be careful. You could be getting into an expensive situation.

- Get the AI supplier to show you a diagram of how your technology system and their AI product will work with each other. If you need to, find a techie colleague who can help walk you through the diagram to check that what is being presented is doable. There are forums on the internet that you can ask questions in. Quora is a good one to check out.

- As with any new software it's important to understand what IT resources the AI product needs to function properly. Ask about these.

- Usually there is some work to be done to integrate existing software with new products. This is just a note to be a bit cautious before signing any contracts.

FACTORS TO CONSIDER

7. Accuracy

Don't be afraid to ask the AI supplier exactly how their product works, in easy to understand language. Take the time to feel comfortable about the answers to any concerns you may have.

Find out what data the product uses and how current it is. Some chatbots have information loaded up to 2 years ago. That might not matter in some contexts, but it's good to know.

Accuracy of the AI results is essential. Ask the supplier what the accuracy rate is and how is it validated? Ask about the issues of *AI Hallucination* and *Catastrophic Forgetting,* where the AI product invents or sometimes just forgets information.

If you're using the AI product in customer service delivery, be sure to check that the information you give the product is, in fact, given out correctly in its responses. Set up a thorough testing program, preferably before you fully commit to buy the product. Ask the AI supplier if you can run the product through some dummy data, so you can evaluate the results. If they say no, that may be a red flag to consider.

After all, it's critical to your business success that your customers receive the correct information, in the right tone for your brand. Taking a zero-tolerance approach to this could save your reputation and your business in the future.

FACTORS TO CONSIDER

8. Security and privacy

IT security is super important for your small business. Ask the AI supplier what level of security and privacy is provided in the product and how are they validated?

What ongoing cyber security protections are there in place and does the AI product meet with data protection regulations?

Do you need to upgrade your business IT security system to cater for the new functionality?

Be aware that any information you put into the AI product, any question, scenario or document may be kept on the product supplier's computers (servers). The AI product learns from every instruction you give it. It may seem cool to have a machine that learns your speaking tone and sounds like you when it writes emails and letters, but as an informed customer, you need to be a little careful what you give to the AI product.

If the information is classified, private, not for public use, or commercial-in-confidence, then it would be a good idea not to give it to the AI product. As this technology matures I expect to see a greater emphasis on the privacy and security of data in AI products.

As a general rule of thumb with AI: *Don't give AI your information if it's not publicly available already and you don't want it to be.*

FACTORS TO CONSIDER

9. Customisation

Most commercial software products are created to accommodate the widest range of customer needs possible. This means that most features provided are generic in nature and built to be configured, not customised. So it follows that customisation is therefore a more expensive route to take.

In all likelihood though your business may have some unique needs, such as catering for a specific customer base and you might require additional data fields, or different types of analytics.

Check with the AI supplier if the product is configurable. An example of this is where the customer can choose to change the field names displayed on the system screens.

If you have to make changes to the hard coding of the AI product be warned that this can be super expensive and take time. It's better to select a product that does 80% of what you need through configuration. Often the easier (and cheaper) solution is to change your business processes to fit the product's structure. I like to think about this as a much-needed housekeeping exercise, where business operations are improved while a new capability is installed.

FACTORS TO CONSIDER

10. Vendor track record

An essential part of your due diligence process is to take the time to check out the AI supplier you're thinking about hiring.

Check their website and talk to people you know about their track record, their experience with AI and their reputation. Keep in mind that the information you find on a company's website will be written with rose-coloured glasses on, but at least it's a starting point.

Look for:

- Reports or articles on the site about the company's involvement with AI.
- Case studies describing actual past customers and how they implemented the AI product.
- Annual reports, if the company has them.
- Testimonials.

Search online for:

- The AI Supplier's competitors.
- Reviews of the AI Supplier's products andservices.
- Check that this company isn't a SCAM - it might be. The AI field is blossoming like the Wild West at the moment and there will be some unfriendly actors in the mix.
- Check informed crowd sources like Quora and AI forums about the company and their product.
- Check out government websites to see if there has been any advice on complaints about the company.

FACTORS TO CONSIDER

11. Uncommon factors

As well as the more common factors to consider when purchasing an AI product, the following is a list of other factors that are worth reviewing and talking to the AI supplier about:

- **Energy efficiency** - AI products are often energy hungry. Will that significantly alter your environmental footprint?

- **Technical requirements** - What are the exact system specifications so you can find out if your hardware and software systems are compatible?

- **Business requirements** - Have you written out exactly what you want the AI product to do for you? Have you created scenarios/use cases so that it's easy to tell the technical folk what you intend to do with the product? See *Chapter 2 Small Business Using AI* for some ideas.

- **Bias detection** - Does the AI product have bias detection built in, to protect you from unintentional discrimination or exclusion?

- **Language support** - If you have multi-lingual settings, can the AI product support that?

- **Integration with legacy systems** - Can the AI product talk to your older systems, and use the data already collected so that trends and customer patterns are kept?

FACTORS TO CONSIDER

- **Open source technologies** - Does the AI product use open source, which can help lower future costs and support new development?
- **Data storage and management** - How does the AI product store data? Is it routinely backed up and is the data stored in an ethical way/location? Is the data appropriately encrypted?
- **Check if you have the following IT plans:**
  - 2-5 Year Business AI Strategy.
  - Data Management Plan.
  - Data Backup Plan.
  - Disaster Recovery Plan.
  - Business Continuity Plan.
  - Privacy Plan.
  - Change Management and Training Plans.
- **Ethical considerations** - Does using the AI product align with your business values? Is it something that you can be transparent with your customers about? If not, why not?
- **Longevity** - Think about the life cycle of the AI product. Is the AI supplier committed to the product for years to come, or are they transitioning to a bigger, more expensive product in the short term?
- **Future proofing** - As your business grows, think about the AI product's ability to adapt to your changed requirements. Will new functionalities, integrations and upgrades be provided by the IT supplier, so that the product will still be as useful to you in 3-5 years as it may be today?

FACTORS TO CONSIDER

12. AI Strategy

As well as the preceding considerations, here are some questions which you might like to think about before selecting an AI product:

- What do you want to accomplish with the AI product? Are you trying to improve efficiency, reduce costs, enhance customer experience, or something else? Your prospective AI supplier should be interested in this.

- Identify the specific problems or pain points that you want an AI product to solve. For example, are you struggling with high customer churn rates, or do you need to automate repetitive tasks?

- How much can you afford to spend on an AI product, and do you have the necessary technical expertise to implement and maintain it?

- How do the available AI products on the market compare against each other? Are they aligned with your business goals and brand?

- Does the AI supplier offer a free trial or demonstration, so that you can run your own process scenarios through the product, as a test?

- Given what you've learned so far, are you prepared to evolve in your AI product journey, as your business needs become more complex? If so, should you create a 2-5 year AI strategy?

MY NOTES

Chapter 9

FINAL CHECKLIST BEFORE YOU BUY AI

BEFORE YOU BUY AI
FINAL CHECKLIST

Use this checklist to help confirm your opinion about an AI product before going ahead with it.

1 **Data privacy and security**: AI products require access to data, and it is important to ensure that the data is secure and protected from unauthorised access.

2 **Bias and fairness**: AI products can be biased if the data used to train them is biased. Ensure that the data used to train AI products is diverse and representative of the population.

3 **Integration and compatibility**: Ensure that the AI product you choose is compatible with your existing IT systems and can be easily integrated into your workflow.

4 **Cost**: AI products can be expensive. Ensure that the cost of the product is justified by the benefits it provides.

5 **Technical expertise**: AI products require technical expertise to set up and maintain. Ensure that you have the necessary technical expertise or can hire someone who does.

6 **Ethical considerations**: Consider the ethical implications of using AI products and ensure that they align with your principles and values.

BEFORE YOU BUY AI
CHECKLIST

7 **Impact on employees**: AI products can automate tasks that were previously done by employees. Consider the impact of AI products on your team.

8 **Accuracy and reliability**: Ensure that the AI product you choose is accurate and reliable. Test the product thoroughly before implementing it to be sure that it will do what you need.

9 **Scalability**: Consider the scalability of the AI product you choose. Ensure that the product can handle not only your current needs but can scale up as your business grows.

10 **User experience**: Consider the user experience of the AI product you choose. Ensure that the product is easy to use and understand, and that it provides a positive experience for your customers.

11 **Legal and regulatory compliance**: Ensure that the AI product you choose complies with all relevant laws and regulations and that you have all the necessary legal agreements in place protecting your IP.

12 **Vendor reputation**: Research the reputation of the vendor of the AI product you choose. Ensure that the vendor has a good track record and is trustworthy.

Keep your dreams alive.

Understand to achieve anything requires faith and belief in yourself, vision, hard work, determination, and dedication.

Remember all things are possible for those who believe.

- Gail Devers

Chapter 10

FEATURES TO LOOK FOR IN SALES & MARKETING AI

10. FEATURES TO LOOK FOR IN SALES & MARKETING AI

In this chapter we'll take a look at the specific AI product types which can greatly enhance small business sales and marketing efforts.

For each AI type (e.g. chatbots) I've included their main features to help you think about which one might be useful for your business.

Each AI type has commonly found bugs, so I've included an overview of them as well so you're aware of what can happen with each AI type.

FEATURES TO LOOK FOR IN SALES & MARKETING AI

1. Chatbots

Here are some features to look for when shopping for a good chatbot to use in sales and marketing:

- Natural Language Processing capabilities to understand and respond to customer inquiries in a conversational manner.
- Ability to handle multiple conversations simultaneously to improve efficiency and response times.
- Multilingual support: Communicate in multiple languages to cater to a diverse customer base.
- Personalisation options to tailor the conversation to the customer's needs and preferences based on the user's behaviour and preferences.
- Integration: Integrate with the business's website, social media platforms, and social messaging platforms.
- Lead Generation: Collect user information and generate leads for the business.
- Analytics and reporting capabilities to track user engagement and identify areas for improvement.

FEATURES TO LOOK FOR IN SALES & MARKETING AI

- Integration with CRM systems to capture and manage leads generated through the chatbot.
- 24/7 availability: Be available 24/7 to cater to customers across different time zones.
- Clear navigation: Provide easy-to-understand prompts to guide users through the sales and marketing funnel.
- Easy customisation and configuration options to adapt to the changing needs of the business over time.

Common chatbot bugs

Here are some common bugs seen in chatbots:

- Poorly designed user interface: If the chatbot's interface is not intuitive or user-friendly, customers may become frustrated and abandon the chat.
- Misunderstanding customer input and providing irrelevant responses.
- Failing to recognise and respond to variations in customer language or phrasing.

FEATURES TO LOOK FOR IN SALES & MARKETING AI

- Technical glitches: If the chatbot experiences slow response times or crashes, it may disrupt customer interactions and damage the business reputation.

- Inability to provide personalised responses or recommendations.

- Lack of integration with other sales and marketing tools or systems.

- Failure to provide accurate information if the chatbot is not updated regularly with the latest product or service information.

- Difficulty handling complex or lengthy customer inquiries or requests. Need a Plan B to quickly triage the customer to a human Customer Service Officer.

FEATURES TO LOOK FOR IN SALES & MARKETING AI

2. Customer Relationship Management (CRM) products

Here are some features to look for when shopping for a good AI CRM product:

- Contact management: ability to manage customer data and interactions in one place.

- Lead management: ability to track and manage leads throughout the sales funnel.

- Marketing automation: ability to automate marketing tasks such as email campaigns, social media posts, and advertising.

- Sales forecasting: ability to predict future sales based on historical data and trends.

- Analytics and reporting: ability to track and measure key metrics such as conversion rates, revenue, and customer acquisition cost.

- Integration with other tools: ability to integrate with other business tools such as email, calendar, and project management.

- Mobile app: ability to access and manage the CRM on-the-go.

- Personalisation: ability to personalise customer interactions and provide tailored recommendations.

FEATURES TO LOOK FOR IN SALES & MARKETING AI

- Customisation and flexibility to fit the specific needs of your business.
- Lead scoring and prioritisation to focus on the most promising sales leads.
- Automated workflows and tasks to streamline sales and marketing processes.
- Collaboration and communication tools for team members to work together effectively.
- Scalability to grow and adapt with your business over time.
- Security features to protect sensitive customer data.

Check that using AI in your CRM isn't violating privacy laws in your location or jurisdiction.

Keeping up to date with changes in privacy legislation will keep you ahead of the game.

FEATURES TO LOOK FOR IN SALES & MARKETING AI

Common CRM bugs

Here are some common bugs seen in AI Customer Relationship Management (CRM) products:

- Data duplication or inaccuracies that can lead to incorrect insights or recommendations.
- System crashes or technical glitches that can interrupt sales and marketing processes.
- Over-reliance on AI recommendations, without human verification, which can lead to missed opportunities or ineffective strategies.
- Inability to integrate with other tools or platforms used by the business, which can lead to manual workarounds and inefficiencies.
- Security vulnerabilities that could lead to data breaches or unauthorised access to sensitive information.
- Incorrectly assigned leads or contacts.
- Poor user interface or user experience.
- Inconsistent or unreliable data syncing.

FEATURES TO LOOK FOR IN SALES & MARKETING AI

- Incorrect or incomplete data mapping.
- Limited customisation options.
- Compatibility issues with certain devices or browsers.
- Lack of integration with other sales and marketing tools or systems, especially chatbots.
- Lack of 24/7 availability.
- Difficult or expensive customisation and configuration options needed to adapt to the changing needs of the business.

FEATURES TO LOOK FOR IN SALES & MARKETING AI

3. Social media AI products

Here are some features to look for when shopping for a good social media AI product to use for sales and marketing:

- Advanced analytics and reporting capabilities to track social media performance and identify areas for improvement.
- Automated content creation and scheduling to save time and increase engagement.
- Personalisation and segmentation options to enable targeted messaging for different audiences.
- Lead generation and lead scoring capabilities to identify potential customers and prioritise follow-up efforts.
- Integration with other marketing and sales tools to streamline workflows and improve collaboration.
- Access to multiple social media platforms to reach a wider audience.
- Customer service and support features to respond to inquiries and comments on social media in a timely manner.

FEATURES TO LOOK FOR IN SALES & MARKETING AI

- AI-powered chatbots for customer service and support to improve response times and customer satisfaction.
- Customisable dashboards and reports to track social media performance and Return on Investment.
- Sentiment analysis to monitor how your brand is perceived on social media.
- Advanced targeting capabilities to reach specific audiences on social media.
- Mobile optimisation to manage social media campaigns on-the-go.

Social media AI can take you to the next level against your competition.

The fastest way to get good results is to spend time planning your social media strategy - Think about what your brand stands for and what business outcomes you want to achieve. Use this information to drive your social media strategy.

FEATURES TO LOOK FOR IN SALES & MARKETING AI

Common social media AI bugs

Here are some common bugs seen in AI social media products:

- Inaccurate data analysis and reporting.
- Poor natural language processing capabilities leading to incorrect sentiment analysis and inappropriate responses to user queries and comments.
- Inability to integrate with other marketing and sales tools.
- Limited language support or inability to cater to diverse audiences.
- Poor recommendation engine leading to ineffective content suggestions and campaign optimisation.
- Poorly targeted advertising campaigns.
- Inconsistent or unreliable performance.
- Lack of customisation or personalisation options.

FEATURES TO LOOK FOR IN SALES & MARKETING AI

- Difficulty in measuring campaign success or Return on Investment.
- Inefficient or slow response times to customer inquiries or complaints.
- Inadequate data security measures.
- Inability to adapt to changes in social media algorithms or trends.

While it's exciting to use AI for your business processes, make sure that you have the necessary legal agreements in place with your AI supplier. This includes a Non-Disclosure Agreement that the supplier won't re-use or redistribute the information that you enter into the product.

FEATURES TO LOOK FOR IN SALES & MARKETING AI

4. Email marketing AI products

Here are some features to look for when shopping for a good AI email marketing product:

- Personalisation capabilities to tailor emails to individual recipients.
- Automated segmentation of email lists based on user behaviour and characteristics.
- Ability to schedule and automate email campaigns.
- A/B split testing functionality to optimise email subject lines, content and calls-to-action.
- Integration with other marketing and sales tools like CRMs and social media platforms.
- Metrics tracking and analysis to measure email campaign effectiveness.
- Spam filter and compliance with email regulations to ensure deliverability and legal compliance with email marketing regulations like GDPR and CAN-SPAM.
- Integration with e-commerce platforms for transactional emails and abandoned cart recovery.

FEATURES TO LOOK FOR IN SALES & MARKETING AI

- Analytics and reporting capabilities to track email performance and Return on Investment.
- User-friendly interface and easy-to-use email template editor.
- Responsive design for mobile devices.
- Support and training resources for smooth implementation and use.

Common email marketing AI bugs

Here are some common bugs seen in AI email marketing products:

- Limited reporting and analytics: Not providing enough data on email performance, making it difficult to optimise email campaigns.
- Poor email deliverability: Not having robust email protocols, causing emails to end up in spam folders or not delivered.
- Inaccurate segmentation: Incorrectly segment contacts, resulting in emails being sent to the wrong customers.

FEATURES TO LOOK FOR IN SALES & MARKETING AI

- Incorrect personalisation: Failing to personalise emails correctly, causing emails to appear spammy or irrelevant.
- Inconsistencies in email formatting: Issues with formatting emails consistently across different email clients and devices.
- Lack of customisation options for email templates and content.
- Difficulties with integrating with other marketing tools and software.
- Inability to handle complex workflows and conditional logic
- Inadequate or unclear customer support and training resources.

FEATURES TO LOOK FOR IN SALES & MARKETING AI

5. AI Personalisation products

Here are some features to look for when shopping for a good AI personalisation product:

- Ability to segment your audience based on different criteria. e.g. demographics, behaviour, interests, prior sales.
- Scheduling automation to send personalised messages at the right time or for special events.
- Integration with your customer relationship management (CRM) system to better track and manage customer interactions.
- A/B split testing capabilities to compare the effectiveness personalised messaging variations.
- Multi-channel support to personalise messaging across various marketing channels. e.g. email, social media, business website.
- Analytics and reporting to measure the success of personalised campaigns and make data-driven decisions for future campaigns.
- Scalability to handle growing customer bases.
- User-friendly interface to make it easy for to use.

FEATURES TO LOOK FOR IN SALES & MARKETING AI

Common AI personalisation product bugs

Here are some common bugs seen in AI personalisation products:

- Inaccurate or incomplete data: If the product is not properly collecting and maintaining customer data, it may not be able to provide accurate personalisation.
- Slow loading times or technical glitches that disrupt the user experience.
- Over-reliance on default templates that do not account for diverse customer needs.
- Limited personalisation options that do not allow for customisation.
- Poor integration with other business products such as a CRM or email marketing automation platform, meaning it may not be able to provide a complete picture of the customer.
- If the product is causing slow load times it can negatively impact the user experience and lead to decreased engagement.

FEATURES TO LOOK FOR IN SALES & MARKETING AI

- Lack of security measures to protect customer data.
- Inconsistent user experience: If the personalisation is not consistent across all touchpoints, it can lead to a confusing and disjointed user experience.

FEATURES TO LOOK FOR IN SALES & MARKETING AI

6. Recommendation engines

Here are some features to look for when shopping for a good recommendation engine:

- Provide tailored recommendations to each individual customer based on their preferences and buying behaviour.

- Scalability to handle increasing amounts of data and customer interactions.

- User-friendly interface and easy integration with existing marketing and sales products.

- Flexibility to adapt to changing customer behaviour and preferences.

- Provide detailed data insights on customer behaviour, preferences, and engagement.

- Multi-channel capabilities to provide recommendations across various platforms and devices.

- Privacy and security features in place to protect customer data and ensure compliance with regulations such as GDPR and CCPA.

- Ability to test and optimise recommendations through A/B split testing and machine learning algorithms.

FEATURES TO LOOK FOR IN SALES & MARKETING AI

Common recommendation engine bugs

Here are some common bugs seen in recommendation engines:

- Inaccurate recommendations due to insufficient data or flawed algorithms.
- Limited product or service options for recommendations.
- Over-reliance on certain types of data, leading to biased recommendations.
- Difficulty integrating with existing sales and marketing systems.
- Insufficient customer data to make accurate recommendations.
- Difficulty in adapting to changes in customer behaviour or business goals.
- Poor performance or slow response time in predicting the outcome of new or untested marketing strategies.
- Inability to handle large amounts of data or scale to meet the needs of a growing business.

FEATURES TO LOOK FOR IN SALES & MARKETING AI

- Lack of transparency in how recommendations are generated.
- Difficulty in customising or adjusting recommendation algorithms.
- Inadequate user training or support for using the product effectively.

FEATURES TO LOOK FOR IN SALES & MARKETING AI

7. AI sentiment analysis products

Here are some features to look for when shopping for a good AI sentiment analysis product:

- The ability to analyse sentiment in real-time, so you can respond quickly to customer feedback and take appropriate action.
- The ability to analyse sentiment in multiple languages, especially if your business operates in a multilingual environment.
- The ability to customise the sentiment analysis model to fit the unique needs of your business, industry, and target audience.
- The ability to accurately identify sentiment, even in complex sentences or with sarcasm, irony, or humour.
- The ability to integrate with other products and platforms, such as social media, email marketing, and customer relationship management (CRM) systems.
- The ability to provide clear and concise reports and dashboards with insights and recommendations for improving customer experience and sales performance.

FEATURES TO LOOK FOR IN SALES & MARKETING AI

- The product should be user-friendly and easy to use.
- The product should be affordable and provide value for money.
- The ability to scale the product as the business grows and the customer base expands.

FEATURES TO LOOK FOR IN SALES & MARKETING AI

Common AI sentiment analysis product bugs

Here are some common bugs in AI sentiment analysis products:

- Inability to identify sentiment in short or informal text.
- Limited vocabulary or inability to understand industry-specific language.
- Over-reliance on keywords instead of analysing the overall context.
- Inaccurate identification of named entities or people mentioned in the text.
- Over-generalisation: When the product applies the same sentiment to all instances of a particular word or phrase, regardless of context.
- Ambiguity: When the product misinterprets the sentiment of a text due to the presence of sarcasm, irony, or humour.
- Biases: When the product exhibits biases towards certain groups of people or types of content, leading to inaccurate sentiment analysis.

FEATURES TO LOOK FOR IN SALES & MARKETING AI

- Inability to detect nuances: When the product fails to detect subtle differences in sentiment, such as between slightly positive and strongly positive statements.

- Limited language support: When the product is unable to analyse sentiment in multiple languages, limiting its usefulness for international business.

FEATURES TO LOOK FOR IN SALES & MARKETING AI

8. AI predictive analytics products

Here are some features to look for when shopping for a good AI predictive analytics product:

- Customisable and flexible data integration to ensure that it can easily integrate with existing products and data sources.

- Ability to generate accurate and actionable insights that are relevant to the business.

- Scalable and can handle increasing amounts of data and customers as the business grows.

- User-friendly interface that allows non-technical users to easily access and interpret the data and insights.

- Advanced analytics capabilities, such as machine learning and natural language processing, to create more accurate predictions and insights.

- Real-time data processing and analysis to respond to changes in the market and customer behaviour quickly.

- Strong security features protecting sensitive data and complying with data privacy regulations.

FEATURES TO LOOK FOR IN SALES & MARKETING AI

Common AI predictive analytics product bugs

Here are some common bugs seen in AI predictive analytics products:

- Overfitting and Underfitting: When the model is too complex or too simple resulting in poor performance.
- Imbalanced data: When the data used to train the model is biased towards a particular outcome, leading to inaccurate predictions.
- Outliers: Data points that are significantly different from the rest of the data and can impact the accuracy of the model.
- Data quality issues: Incomplete, inconsistent, or inaccurate data that can negatively affect the performance of the model.
- Bias in the data or the model that may skew the results.
- Poor data visualisation or reporting capabilities.
- Unreliable or inconsistent performance of the tool over time.

FEATURES TO LOOK FOR IN SALES & MARKETING AI

- Lack of transparency: The model should be explainable and transparent, so that users can understand how predictions are made.

- Limited scope of the product, leading to incomplete insights.

FEATURES TO LOOK FOR IN SALES & MARKETING AI

9. AI cyber security products

Here are some features to look for when shopping for a good AI cyber security product:

- Real-time threat detection and response capabilities using behavioural analysis capabilities to detect unusual activity.
- Phishing and spam protection to prevent social engineering and denial of service attacks.
- Encryption and data loss prevention features to protect sensitive information.
- Advanced analytics and reporting to monitor cyber threats and vulnerabilities.
- Integration with existing security systems and platforms for a more comprehensive defence.
- User-friendly interface and ease of use.
- Automated updates and security patch management to ensure the product is always current.
- Ability to provide granular access controls and permissions to ensure data privacy and security.
- User activity monitoring to track and manage access to critical systems and data.

FEATURES TO LOOK FOR IN SALES & MARKETING AI

Common AI cyber security product bugs

Here are some common bugs seen in AI cyber security products:

- False positives: The product may flag legitimate activity as suspicious or potentially malicious.
- False negatives: The product may miss actual security threats.
- Inadequate threat detection: The product may not identify all security threats, such as malware, phishing, and unauthorised access.
- Limited coverage: The product may not cover all areas of the business, leaving some systems or data vulnerable.
- Poor integration: The product may not work well with other security products or business processes, causing gaps in the security infrastructure.
- High maintenance: The product may require frequent manual updates, making it costly to keep up to date.
- Insufficient reporting: The product may not provide enough information or insights to help businesses make informed decisions about their security posture.

MY NOTES

Chapter 11

COMMON
AI BUGS

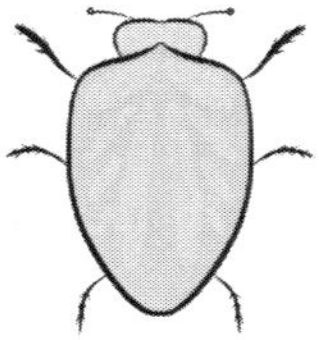

11. COMMON AI BUGS

As with all software programs, AI products are prone to various problems, known in the industry as *bugs*. Some are small and easily fixed and others not so.

To further your education as an *Informed Customer*, I've added this section to show you the most common AI bugs and their suggested preventative measures.

Please don't worry that you have to understand and apply these techniques. Most of the bugs will need a technical AI specialist, usually provided by your AI supplier, to fix them.

The objective of this section is to raise your awareness about the problems that can happen with AI. It is good to remember that the AI industry is still in its infancy and bugs are bound to occur. Only time working with the products will smooth them out.

So, when you talk with AI suppliers and especially later, when you're implementing your selected AI product, hopefully you'll feel better prepared having read through this section. Particularly when that discussion is with a technical specialist trying to resolve your AI issue.

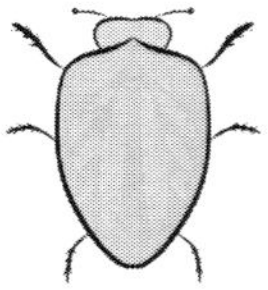

COMMON AI BUGS

1. AI hallucination

AI hallucination occurs when a machine learning model generates outputs that are not consistent with the input data or the real-world context. This means that the model is generating outputs that are not based on the actual patterns in the data, but rather on spurious correlations or noise in the data.

It can be caused by several factors, including the architecture of the model, the quality of the training data, or the complexity of the problem being solved.

Common preventative measures are regularisation, data cleaning, or model interpretability.

2. Catastrophic forgetting

Catastrophic forgetting occurs when a machine learning model learns new data and it overwrites or forgets previously learned data. This results in poorer performance on tasks that require facts from multiple domains.

It can be caused by several factors, including the architecture of the model, the learning rate, or the order in which the data is presented to the model.

Common preventative measures are regularisation, rehearsal, or fine-tuning.

COMMON AI BUGS

3. Data bias

Data bias occurs when a reflection of underlying societal or historical biases present in the data, result in inaccurate or discriminatory predictive outcomes.

It can be caused by several factors, including the data collection process, the sampling strategy used to create the training data, or the presence of confounding variables that are correlated with the target variable.

Common preventative measures are to carefully curate the training data and to use data augmentation, data cleaning, and fairness constraints.

4. Data leakage

Data leakage occurs when the training and testing datasets are not properly separated and there is an overlap between them leading to artificially inflated performance metrics. In regards to security, data leakage occurs when an AI model is trained on sensitive data, and the model inadvertently reveals that data to unauthorised parties.

This can happen if the model is not properly secured or if there are vulnerabilities in the system that allow unauthorised access to the model or the data it uses.

Common preventative measures are to ensure proper separation of training, development, test data, and consider data anonymisation techniques, together with appropriate role-based security access.

COMMON AI BUGS

5. Overfitting

Overfitting occurs when a machine learning model is trained too well on a specific dataset. This means that the model has learned the data so well that it starts to memorise it instead of generalising it. As a result, the model performs poorly on new data that it has not seen before.

Common preventative measures are regularisation, cross-validation, and early stopping. More diverse training data and a smaller network size can also help.

6. Underfitting

Underfitting occurs when a machine learning model is too simple to capture the complexity of the data. This means that the model is not able to learn the patterns in the data and performs poorly on both the training and test data.

Common preventative measures are using a more complex model, increasing the number of features, or increasing the training time. Alternatively, using an ensemble of different models can help increase accuracy.

COMMON AI BUGS

7. Vanishing gradients

Vanishing gradients occur during the training of deep neural networks. It happens when the gradients of the loss function become very small as they propagate through the network during back-propagation. This means that the weights of the network are not being updated properly, and the network is not learning effectively.

Common preventative measures are to use activation functions that have larger gradients and to use techniques such as weight initialisation, batch normalisation, and gradient clipping.

8. Exploding gradients

Exploding gradients occur during the training of deep neural networks. It happens when the gradients of the loss function become very large as they propagate through the network during back-propagation. This means that the weights of the network are being updated too much, and the network is not learning effectively.

Common preventative measures are gradient clipping, weight regularisation, and batch normalisation.

COMMON AI BUGS

9. Adversarial attacks

Adversarial attacks occur when an attacker intentionally manipulates the input data to a machine learning model in order to cause it to misclassify the data. Adversarial attacks can be performed by adding small perturbations to the input data that are imperceptible to humans but can cause the model to make incorrect predictions.

Adversarial attacks can be a serious problem for machine learning models, especially those used in security-critical applications such as autonomous vehicles or medical diagnosis.

Common preventative measures are adversarial training, input sanitisation, and model verification.

10. Label noise

Label noise occurs when the labels in the training data are incorrect or noisy. This means that the model is being trained on data that is not representative of the true labels, which can lead to poor performance on new data.

Label noise can be caused by several factors, including human error in labeling the data, errors in data collection or preprocessing, or intentional manipulation of the data.

Common preventative measures are to ensure the quality of the labeled data, collect more high-quality data-points, and use error-correcting codes to mitigate the effect.

COMMON AI BUGS

11. Class imbalance

Class imbalance occurs when the distribution of classes in the training data is uneven. This means that one or more classes have significantly fewer examples than the others, which can lead to poor performance on the under-represented classes.

Class imbalance can be caused by several factors, including the nature of the problem being solved, the data collection process, or the sampling strategy used to create the training data.

Common preventative measures are oversampling, undersampling, or class weighting.

12. Covariate shift

Covariate shift occurs when the distribution of the input data changes between the training and test phases. This means that the model is being trained on data that is different from the data it will encounter during deployment, which can lead to poor performance on new data.

Covariate shift can be caused by several factors, including changes in the data collection process, changes in the environment or context in which the model is deployed, or changes in the user behaviour or preferences.

Common preventative measures are domain adaptation, importance weighting, or data augmentation.

COMMON AI BUGS

13. Unreliable feedback data

Unreliable feedback data occurs when the data used to train an AI model contains errors, leading to incorrect action predictions. This means that the model is being trained or evaluated on data that does not reflect its true performance.

Unreliable feedback data can be caused by several factors, including human error in labeling the data, errors in data collection or preprocessing, or intentional manipulation of the data.

Common preventative measures are to collect more high quality data and use techniques such as inter-rater reliability, data cleaning, or crowdsourcing.

14. Outliers

Outliers refer to data points that are significantly different from other data points in a dataset. Outliers can become a bug in AI when they're not properly handled or accounted for in the training of a machine learning model.

Outliers can skew the results of a model, leading to inaccurate predictions or classifications.

Common preventative measures are to filter them from the dataset before training the model, particularly in supervised learning. Other methods used are winsorisation, clustering, robust regression or data transformation.

COMMON AI BUGS

15. Lack of interpretability

Lack of interpretability occurs when a machine learning model is not able to provide explanations for its predictions or decisions. This means that it is difficult to understand why certain decisions were made.

Simpler algorithms that are easier to interpret such as Feature Importance, Partial Dependence Plots, LIME and SHAP values, can be used to explain the results and decision-making patterns of AI models.

Common preventative measures are model interpretability, feature importance, or attention mechanisms.

16. Computationally expensive models

Computationally expensive models occur when the machine learning model is too complex and requires a large amount of computer processing resources to train, maintain, use or scale. This means that the model is impractical for use in real-world applications.

Common preventative measures are model compression, approximate computation, transfer learning, or hardware acceleration.

MY NOTES

The moment one definitely commits oneself,

then Providence moves too.

Whatever you think you can do,

or believe you can do, begin it.

Action has magic, power and grace.

- Johann Wolfgang von Goethe

Chapter 12

MEASURING YOUR AI INVESTMENT

12. MEASURING YOUR AI INVESTMENT

At this point I need to mention that I'm not a qualified financial professional. Before making any business decisions you should seek accredited professional advice.

However, to help you achieve success with AI, I felt it was important to include some basic information on ROI so that you can start thinking about how you're going to apply the concept in your business.

Measuring the return on investment (ROI) of AI products is crucial for small business because it helps you to work out if the AI product has been successful in boosting your business performance, or not.

The sooner you work this out, the quicker you can decide if you need to stop the exercise before wasting more money if it isn't worth the investment. Or conversely, allocate more funding to a successful trial period.

MEASURING YOUR AI INVESTMENT

The easiest way to measure the ROI of your AI products, is to track the key performance indicators (KPIs) relevant to your business goals.

Once you have identified your relevant KPIs, you can use your AI tools to track and analyse the data. Many AI tools come with built-in analytics and reporting features that can help you measure the impact of your marketing and sales efforts.

To calculate the ROI of your AI tools, you will need to compare the cost of the tool to the revenue generated or cost savings achieved as a result of using the tool.

EXAMPLE
If you spend $1,000 on an AI tool and it helps you generate $5,000 in additional revenue, then your ROI would be 400%.

It's important to note that measuring the ROI of AI tools can be complex, and it may be helpful to work with a data analyst, an accountant or marketing consultant to ensure that you are tracking and interpreting the right data for your business needs.

The KPIs you track will depend on your specific business goals and marketing strategy. It's important to choose KPIs that are relevant to your business, that you can realistically track and measure over time.

MEASURING YOUR AI INVESTMENT

ROI formula

To calculate the Return on Investment (ROI) for an AI implementation in a small business, you can use the following formula:

ROI = (Net Profit from AI - Investment Cost) / Investment Cost * 100

Here's a breakdown of the components of the formula:

1. Net Profit from AI: Calculate the additional net profit generated as a result of implementing the AI solution. This includes any increase in revenue or cost savings directly attributed to the AI product. Subtract any additional expenses incurred due to the AI implementation.

Net Profit from AI = Additional Revenue - Additional Expenses

2. Investment Cost: Determine the total cost associated with acquiring and implementing the AI product. This includes upfront costs such as software licenses, hardware, training, customisation, and any ongoing expenses like maintenance or subscription fees.

3. Calculate the difference between Net Profit from AI and Investment Cost.

4. Divide the difference by the Investment Cost.

5. Multiply the result by 100 to convert it into a percentage.

NOTE: Remember to check your calculations with your financial professional before committing any money.

MEASURING YOUR AI INVESTMENT

The resulting ROI percentage indicates the efficiency and profitability of the AI investment.

A positive ROI percentage means the investment is generating more profit than the cost incurred, indicating a favourable return.

Conversely, a negative ROI percentage implies that the AI investment is not generating sufficient returns.

EXAMPLES

1. If your goal is to increase sales, then the KPIs to track might include the number of leads generated, the conversion rate of those leads into customers, the average revenue per customer or the life time value of the customer.

2. If your goal is to improve marketing efficiency, then the KPIs to track might include the cost per lead, the cost per acquisition, and the return on ad spend.

It's important to note that ROI calculations for AI implementation may include considering other factors specific to your business, such as your timeframe for measuring returns and the expected life cycle of your particular AI product.

Adjust the formula and factors as necessary to tailor it to your unique business circumstances.

MEASURING YOUR AI INVESTMENT

Key performance indicator types

Here are some common Key Performance Indicators to measure the ROI on AI products:

1. Customer Lifetime Value (CLV): This metric measures the total amount of revenue a customer is expected to generate over the course of their relationship with your business. Tracking the CLV, you can identify which customers are most valuable to your business and focus your marketing efforts on retaining and upselling to them.

2. Customer Acquisition Cost (CAC): This metric measures the cost of acquiring a new customer. By tracking the CAC, you can identify which marketing channels and campaigns are most effective at driving new business, and adjust your strategy accordingly.

3. Website Traffic: This metric measures the number of visitors to your website. By tracking website traffic, you can identify which marketing channels and campaigns are driving the most traffic to your site, and adjust your strategy accordingly.

4. Conversion Rate: This metric measures the percentage of website visitors who take a desired action, such as making a purchase or filling out a lead form. By tracking conversion rate, you can identify which pages and campaigns are most effective at driving conversions, and adjust your strategy accordingly.

MEASURING YOUR AI INVESTMENT

5. Social Media Engagement: This metric measures the number of likes, comments, shares, and other interactions your social media posts receive. By tracking social media engagement, you can identify which types of content and messaging resonate most with your audience, and adjust your social media strategy accordingly.

6. Email Open and Click-Through Rates: These metrics measure the percentage of email recipients who open your emails and click on links within them. By tracking email open and click-through rates, you can identify which subject lines, messaging, and calls-to-action are most effective at engaging your audience, and adjust your email marketing strategy accordingly.

7. Track Sales: AI products can help small businesses better understand customers' shopping habits, preferences, and orders. By tracking sales and comparing them to past data, small businesses can determine if there has been improved sales growth due to the implementation of AI products.

8. Customer Retention: One of the key metrics for ROI is customer retention. By measuring customer retention rates, businesses can analyse if AI tools improve customer interactions, satisfaction, and loyalty. Measuring the customer acquisition rate vs. retention rate can be a good indication of the customer satisfaction level.

MEASURING YOUR AI INVESTMENT

9. **Support Cost Savings**: Chatbots can help businesses save on support costs by automating routine queries, enabling human agents to focus on complex tasks. Comparing support costs before and after implementing AI products can indicate how much small businesses are saving through automation.

10. **Efficiency**: AI products can help small business owners automate tasks, reducing human errors and increasing efficiency. Measuring the time taken to complete tasks before and after AI implementation can indicate whether there has been an increase in efficiency and reduced turnaround time.

11. **Cost Reduction**: AI products can help reduce operational costs from staff training, overhead expenses, and technical support to additional software or hardware costs. With AI tools enabling small businesses to streamline their operations, the cost savings can be significant.

12. **Surveys and Feedback**: Integrating customer feedback and surveys to collect data on customer experience and satisfaction can also help small businesses to measure the ROI of AI products. Positive feedback and an increase in customer satisfaction can indicate that the AI tool has been effective in supporting the business's marketing and sales goals.

By tracking these metrics, you can make informed decisions on whether to continue investing in AI and if you need to re-evaluate your AI strategy.

MEASURING YOUR AI INVESTMENT

Important considerations

To measure the ROI on AI products, keep these things in mind:

1. Define Clear Objectives: Before implementing an AI product, establish specific and measurable goals. Determine what you aim to achieve, such as cost savings, increased productivity, improved customer satisfaction, or revenue growth. Clear objectives provide a basis for measuring ROI.

2. Identify Key Performance Indicators (KPIs): Select relevant metrics that align with your objectives. For example, if your goal is to increase sales, KPIs could include conversion rates, average order value, or customer acquisition cost. Define these KPIs to track and measure the impact of AI on your business.

3. Baseline Measurement: Before implementing an AI product, establish a baseline measurement of the selected KPIs. This provides a reference point for comparison and helps determine the AI product's effectiveness in driving desired outcomes.

4. Track Data: Implement robust tracking systems to collect data related to the chosen KPIs. AI products often generate large amounts of data, which can be analysed to assess their impact. Ensure data accuracy, consistency, and security throughout the tracking process.

MEASURING YOUR AI INVESTMENT

5. Compare Before and After: Once the AI product is implemented, compare the performance of the selected KPIs before and after its introduction. Analyse the difference in metrics to determine the product's impact on your business outcomes.

6. Calculate ROI: Calculate the return on investment by comparing the costs associated with implementing and maintaining the AI product against the benefits achieved. Consider factors such as upfront costs, ongoing expenses, and the time frame for realising the benefits. ROI can be expressed as a percentage or a monetary value.

7. Consider Tangible and Intangible Benefits: AI products may generate both tangible and intangible benefits. Tangible benefits are quantifiable, such as cost savings or revenue growth, while intangible benefits are more subjective, like improved customer satisfaction or brand perception. Assess and include both types of benefits in your ROI analysis.

8. Evaluate Time and Cost Savings: Assess the time and cost savings resulting from the implementation of AI products. Compare the efficiencies gained, reduction in manual labour, or automation of repetitive tasks. Quantifying these savings results in a comprehensive ROI assessment.

9. Conduct Customer Surveys or Feedback Analysis: Gather customer feedback to gauge their satisfaction with the AI product's impact on their experiences. Conduct surveys, analyse sentiment analysis, or track customer reviews to understand the qualitative impact of AI on customer perceptions and loyalty.

10. Regularly Review and Optimise: Continuously monitor and review the AI product's performance and its impact on ROI. Identify areas for improvement and optimisation. Regularly reassess objectives and KPIs to ensure alignment with changing business needs.

In summary

Measuring the ROI of AI products requires a combination of quantitative and qualitative analysis. By diligently tracking data, comparing performance, and considering both tangible and intangible benefits, you can assess the true value and effectiveness of your AI investments.

MEASURING YOUR AI INVESTMENT

How to measure KPIs

To measure Key Performance Indicators (KPIs) related to AI products, consider the following steps:

1. **Data Collection**: Ensure that you have robust data collection systems in place. This may involve integrating AI systems with your existing analytics tools, CRM platforms, or other relevant data sources. Capture and store relevant data points that align with your chosen KPIs.

2. **Data Analysis**: Analyse the collected data to extract meaningful insights. Use statistical methods, data visualisation techniques, or AI-powered analytics tools to identify trends, patterns, and correlations. This analysis will provide a deeper understanding of how the AI product is impacting your KPIs.

3. **KPI Tracking**: Set up a centralised dashboard or reporting system to track your KPIs. This allows you to monitor the metrics in real-time and provides visibility into the performance of the AI product. Regularly update and review this dashboard to stay informed about the progress towards your objectives.

4. **Comparative Analysis**: Compare the KPIs before and after the implementation of the AI product. This involves analysing historical data to establish a baseline measurement and then tracking the changes after the AI product is deployed. Assess the magnitude of the impact and the direction of the change (positive or negative).

MEASURING YOUR AI INVESTMENT

5. A/B Testing: Consider conducting A/B tests to evaluate the effectiveness of the AI product. Split your audience or operations into two groups - one with the AI product and another without, and compare the outcomes. This controlled experiment helps isolate the impact of the AI product and provides insights into its specific contribution.

6. Customer Surveys and Feedback: Supplement quantitative data with qualitative feedback from customers. Implement surveys, feedback forms, or conduct interviews to gather insights about customer experiences and perceptions. Use sentiment analysis tools to analyse customer sentiments expressed in reviews or social media posts.

7. Cohort Analysis: Segment your customer base or operational units into different cohorts and track KPIs within each segment. This analysis helps identify which segments are experiencing the most significant impact from the AI product. By understanding the variations in performance across different cohorts, you can tailor marketing strategies accordingly.

8. Time Frame Considerations: Define the time frame for measuring KPIs based on the nature of your business and the expected impact of the AI product. Short-term KPIs can provide immediate feedback, while long-term KPIs may require more time to manifest results. Adjust the time frame as needed to gain a comprehensive understanding of the AI product's impact.

MEASURING YOUR AI INVESTMENT

9. **Continuous Monitoring and Optimisation**: Regularly monitor KPIs and reassess the effectiveness of the AI product. Identify areas for improvement or optimisation and make necessary adjustments. Continuously update your AI strategy to align with changing business needs and market dynamics.

By following these steps, you can establish a systematic approach to measure and track KPIs related to your AI products. This data-driven evaluation will provide valuable insights into the impact of AI on your business and guide your future decision-making.

GLOSSARY

GLOSSARY

A/B testing - Often called split testing, is an assessment tool for identifying which version of something helps a business meet a specific goal more effectively. A/B testing is commonly used in web development to test which elements resonate better with the audience.

Active Directory - A directory service by Microsoft that allows for centralised authentication and authorisation services for network resources.

Active Learning - A type of machine learning where the algorithm actively selects the most informative training instances for labeling to improve its performance.

Agile - A methodology used in software development that emphasises flexibility, adaptability, and frequent iterations to improve outcomes.

Algorithm - A set of instructions designed to solve a specific problem.

API (Application Programming Interface) - A set of protocols, routines, and tools used to build software and allow applications to interact with each other.

Artificial Intelligence (AI) - A field of computer science focused on creating machines that can perform tasks that normally require human intelligence.

Association Rule Mining - A data mining technique used to find associations or correlations among sets of items in a large database.

Autoencoder - A type of neural network that learns to compress and reconstruct data, useful for tasks such as image or audio compression and de-noising.

Automated Lead Qualification - A process of using AI to automatically qualify leads based on predefined criteria, freeing up salesperson's time to focus on higher priority leads.

Automation - The use of technology to automate workflows and processes traditionally done by humans.

Backpropagation - An algorithm used in neural networks to update the weights of the connections between nodes during training.

Batch Learning - A type of machine learning where the algorithm is trained on batches of data and is updated incrementally as new data comes in.

Batch Normalisation - A technique in deep learning used to adjust and standardise the input values of each layer to improve model performance.

GLOSSARY

Big Data - A term used to describe extremely large data sets that require advanced computing and analysis to uncover insights.

Blockchain - A distributed ledger technology that enables secure and transparent transactions between parties without the need for intermediaries.

Business Intelligence - A set of tools and processes that use data to understand business performance and derive insights to drive decision-making.

Chatbot - A conversational AI tool that can assist with customer service, sales, and engagement.

Cloud AI Services - A suite of cloud-based services provided by major cloud providers such as AWS, Google Cloud Platform, and Microsoft Azure that allow users to build, deploy, and manage AI applications.

Cloud Computing - Delivering computing services over the internet, including storage, servers, databases, networking, and software.

Cloud Storage - A cloud-based data storage service that allows users to store and access their data anytime, anywhere. (see Cloud AI Services)

Computer Vision - A tool that enables computers to analyse and make sense of images and videos, including object recognition, image segmentation, and motion detection. It has a wide range of applications, including self-driving cars, facial recognition, medical imaging, and more.

Convex Optimization - A technique used to find the minimum value of a convex function by optimising its parameters over a convex set of feasible solutions.

Convolutional Neural Networks - A type of neural network that is primarily used for image recognition and processing.

Customer Journey Mapping - A process of visualising the customer's experience across various touch points to improve customer satisfaction and business outcomes.

Customer Relationship Management - A software tool that helps businesses manage their interactions with customers and potential customers. It typically includes features such as contact management, sales management, marketing automation, and customer service and support.

Customer Segmentation - The process of dividing customers into groups based on common characteristics, behaviours, or demographics.

GLOSSARY

Customer Support - The level of support and assistance provided by the AI product developer to the business using the product.

Cybersecurity - The practice of protecting computers, servers, mobile devices, electronic systems, networks, and data from digital attacks or unauthorised access.

Data Analysis - A process of examining and interpreting data to extract insights and knowledge.

Data Annotation - The process of labeling data for training machine learning models or for other analytical purposes.

Data Cleansing - The process of detecting and correcting or removing corrupt, inaccurate, or irrelevant data from a dataset.

Data Leakage - Occurs when the training and testing datasets are not properly separated and there is an overlap between them leading to artificially inflated performance metrics. In regards to security, data leakage occurs when an AI model is trained on sensitive data, and the model inadvertently reveals that data to unauthorised parties.

Data Management - The process of collecting, storing, organizing, maintaining, and utilising data to ensure data quality, integrity, and availability for analysis and decision-making.

Data Mining - The process of discovering patterns and insights in large data sets using statistical and computational methods.

Data Privacy - The practice of protecting sensitive or private information from unauthorised access, disclosure, or misuse.

Data Science for Business - A holistic approach to applying data science and analytics to solve critical business problems, drive innovation, and boost bottom-line performance.

Data Warehousing - The process of collecting, storing, and managing large-scale datasets for business intelligence and analytics purposes.

Decision Support Systems - A type of AI system that helps decision-makers in solving problems by utilising data, models, and algorithms.

Decision Trees - A tree-based model used for classification or regression tasks that splits data into smaller subgroups based on features until a final outcome is determined.

Deep Learning - A form of machine learning that involves training neural networks with multiple layers to find patterns in data.

Dimensionality Reduction - A technique used to reduce the number of variables or features in a dataset to simplify machine learning models or to visualise high-dimensional datasets.

GLOSSARY

Dropout - A technique used in neural networks to randomly drop out some of the connections between nodes during training to prevent overfitting.

Ease of use - How easy or intuitive an AI product is to use.

Edge Computing - A distributed computing architecture that allows computing to occur closer to the source of the data to improve latency, bandwidth, and security.

Ensemble Learning - A technique that combines multiple machine learning models to improve overall predictive power and reduce variance.

Ethics - The moral principles and values that govern the use of AI technology in business and society.

Expert Systems - A type of AI system that emulates the decision-making ability of a human expert in a specific domain.

Feature Engineering - The process of selecting and extracting relevant data features to use for training machine learning models.

Federated Learning - A privacy-preserving machine learning approach where models are trained on locally held data and then updated/re-fitted to the central model.

F1 Score - A metric in machine learning that combines precision and recall to measure the effectiveness of a model.

Generative Adversarial Networks - A type of deep learning model that involves two neural networks that compete with each other to generate realistic data.

Genetic Algorithms - A computational optimisation technique that uses evolutionary principles to find optimised solutions to problems.

GPT (Generative Pre-trained Transformer) - A deep learning algorithm that utilises the Transformer architecture for natural language processing tasks such as language modeling, text generation, and question answering.

Gradient Descent - An optimisation algorithm used in machine learning to find the optimal parameters of a model by minimising the error of the predictions.

Hyperparameter Tuning - The process of selecting optimal hyperparameters for machine learning models to improve their performance.

Hyperparameters - Settings that are predefined before machine learning algorithms are trained and are used to control the training process.

GLOSSARY

Image Recognition - A technique in computer vision that allows machines to recognise and classify images.

Inference - The process of applying a trained machine learning model to new, unseen data to make predictions or findings.

Integration - The ability of an AI product to work seamlessly with existing software and technology used by a business.

IoT (Internet of Things) - A network of interconnected objects that can collect and exchange data.

Keras - A high-level neural network application programming interface (API) in Python that simplifies and speeds up the creation of deep learning models.

KPI (Key Performance Indicator) - A measurable value that demonstrates how effectively a business meets its objectives.

Lead Scoring - A process of assigning scores to leads based on their interests, behaviours, and demographics to prioritise sales efforts.

Machine Learning - A subset of AI that involves training machines to learn from data, without being explicitly programmed to do so.

Natural Language Generation - A subset of Natural Language Processing that involves the creation of natural language text by machine learning models.

Natural Language Processing - A branch of AI that deals with the interaction between humans and computers using natural language.

Natural Language Processing Toolkit (NLTK) - A popular open-source toolset for NLP in Python that provides various libraries and datasets for text processing, tokenisation, and parsing.

Natural Language Querying - A technique that allows users to interact with databases and data analytics systems using natural language phrases.

Network Security - The practice of protecting computer networks from unauthorised access, misuse or disruption, as well as ensuring data confidentiality, integrity, and availability.

Network Topology - The structure of a network and the arrangement of its components, such as nodes and connections.

Neural Network - A type of machine learning model that is structured like the human brain and uses layers of interconnected nodes to learn and draw conclusions from data.

One-shot Learning - A type of machine learning where a model is trained on a single example of each class, allowing it to recognise new samples of these classes.

GLOSSARY

Online Learning - A type of machine learning where the algorithm is trained on data as it arrives in a continuous stream.
Open-Source - A form of software development where the source code is freely available and can be modified and redistributed by anyone.
Overfitting - A common problem in machine learning where a model becomes too complex and fits to the training data too closely, leading to poor performance with new data.
Parallel Computing - A type of computing architecture that allows multiple processors to work together to solve computational problems faster and more efficiently
Personalisation - A marketing strategy that involves tailoring messages and offerings to individual customers based on their interests, preferences, history, and behaviours.
Personalised Product Recommendations - An AI tool that suggests products or services based on a customer's individual preferences, behaviours, and purchase history.
Precision - A metric in machine learning that measures the proportion of true positives in relation to all positive predictions.
Predictive Analytics - The use of statistical and machine learning modeling techniques to analyse data and forecast future outcomes.
Probabilistic Programming - A technique that allows for the creation and training of probabilistic models using a programming language.
PyTorch - An open-source deep learning framework that provides Python-based tensor computation.
Quantum Computing - A new computing paradigm that uses quantum mechanics to perform computations that are infeasible with classical computers.
Recall - A metric in machine learning that measures the proportion of true positives in relation to all positive instances in the data.
Recurrent Neural Networks - A type of neural network that is ideal for processing sequential data and is used in natural language processing and speech recognition.
Reinforcement Learning - A type of machine learning that involves training an algorithm to maximise rewards gained from taking certain actions in an environment.

GLOSSARY

Reinforcement Learning Toolbox (RL Toolbox) - A MATLAB-based toolbox for reinforcement learning that provides a set of algorithms, tools, and visualisation modules for building and testing RL agents.
Robotics - The field of engineering and computer science that is focused on the design, development, and application of robots.
Sales Prediction - The use of AI to make predictions about future sales based on past data and customer behaviour.
Scalability - The ability of an AI product to grow and adapt with a business as it expands.
Scikit-learn - A popular Python library for machine learning that provides easy-to-use and efficient tools for data analysis and model building.
Security - The measures taken to protect AI systems and data from unauthorised access, theft, and manipulation.
Semi-Supervised Learning - A type of machine learning that involves training an algorithm on both labeled and unlabeled data to improve performance.
Sentiment Analysis - A technique in natural language processing that analyses text to determine the emotion (feeling) behind it.
Supervised Learning - A type of machine learning that involves training an algorithm on labeled data to make predictions on new data.
Support Vector Machines - A binary classification algorithm that identifies the optimal decision boundary between classes using a maximal margin hyperplane.
TensorFlow - A popular open-source library for deep learning that provides abstractions for building and training complex neural networks.
Time Series Analysis - A statistical technique used to analyse time-based data to identify patterns and make predictions.
Transfer Function - A mathematical function used to map an input signal to an output signal in artificial neural networks.
Transfer Learning - A process of transferring knowledge from one domain to another to improve performance on a specific task.
Trust and Security - Refers to the level of trustworthiness of the AI product and the security measures in place to protect the business using the product and its customers.

GLOSSARY

Underfitting - A common problem in machine learning where a model is too simple to capture the complexity of the data, leading to poor performance on both the training and new data.

Unsupervised Learning - A type of machine learning that involves training an algorithm on unlabeled data to draw inferences and discover patterns.

User Experience Design - The process of designing digital products that are easy to use, effective, and satisfying for the user of the software (The User).

User Story - A user story is a short, simple description of the functionality of a product or service from the perspective of the customer. It includes a description of the customer, their desired goals and the benefit or value that they'll receive.

When obstacles arise,
you change your direction
to reach your goal -

You do not change your
decision to get there.

- Zig Ziglar

INDEX

INDEX

INDEX

INDEX

REFERENCES

REFERENCES

1. Agbai, C., Lorandi, J.P. (2023). *The power of generative AI: A complete guide for business.* https://www.azumo.com/insights/the-power-of-generative-ai-a-complete-guide-for-business?fbclid=IwAR0GdebSw1laD2_R50nk0sXP0YCL9OgmeuTDy3IV6kInbx3hDH69GS7cxX

2. Blockchain Council. (2023) *Machine learning vs artificial intelligence.* https://www.blockchain-council.org/ai/machine-learning-vs-artificial-intelligence/

3. Bughin, J. and Hazan, E. (2017) *Five management strategies for getting the most from AI.* https://www.mckinsey.com/mgi/overview/in-the-news/five-management-strategies-for-getting-the-most-from-ai

4. ChatGPT. (2023) https://chat.openai.com

5. Course Hero. (n.d.) *What is customer segmentation?* https://www.coursehero.com/file/47688666/ENCS6042-TA-notes-week-3pdf/

6. Course Hero. (n.d.) *Write about computer security in 5 pages.* https://www.coursehero.com/file/188079450/computer-securitydocx/

7. Deloitte. (2019) *The path to prosperity: Why the future of work is human.* https://www2.deloitte.com/us/en/insights/focus/technology-and-the-future-of-work/building-the-lucky-country.html?id=us:2el:3dc:4diAU22531:5awa:6di:fow&pkid=1006529

REFERENCES

8. Favor. (2023) *The future of SAP: Emerging trends and technologies.* favor.com.ua/blogs/36067.html?export=pdf

9. Future Learn. (n.d.) *AI and creative industries.* https://www.futurelearn.com/info/courses/introduction-to-creative-ai/0/steps/95578?main-nav-submenu=main-nav-categories

10. Gartner. (2022) *2022-2024 Technology adoption roadmap for midsize enterprises.* https://www.gartner.com/en/publications/technology-adoption-roadmap-for-midsize-enterprises

11. Gartner. (2022) *Gartner® Magic Quadrant™ for Cloud AI Developer Services report.* https://www.cloud.google.com/resources/2022-gartner-magic-quadrant-cloud-ai-developer-services-report

12. GeeksForGeeks. (n.d.) *Artificial intelligence - An introduction.* https://www.geeksforgeeks.org/artificial-intelligence-an-introduction/amp/?ref=rp

13. Gitnux. (2023) *Data loss prevention strategies exposed - Guide 2023.* blog.gitnux.com/strategies/data-loss-prevention-strategies/

14. Instituto Perfil. (2022) *How to do natural language processing.* https://instituto.perfil.com/rxz/how-to-do-natural-language-processing

15. Intellipaat. (2023)*What is Google Cloud Platform Security?* intellipaat.com/blog/what-is-gcp-security/

REFERENCES

16. Kaur, B. (2023) *Using AI for SEO: Tips, tools, and strategies.* https://www.wordtune.com/blog/using-ai-for-seo-tips-tools-and-strategies

17. Maddison, L. (2023) *Samsung workers made a major error by using ChatGPT.* https://www.techradar.com/news/samsung-workers-leaked-company-secrets-by-using-chatgpt

18. Mintchell, G. (2017) *Practical advice for building industrial Internet of Things.* https://themanufacturingconnection.com/tag/open-standards/page/3/

19. Mizrahi, L. (2023). *Machine learning specialization course.* https://github.com/lironmiz/machine-learning-specialization-course

20. Morgan Kaufman. (2016) *Big data principles and paradigms.* http://www.csce.uark.edu/~lz006/course/2022fall/Big%20Data%20Principles%20and%20Paradigms.pdf

21. OpenGenus. (2023). *50+Key terms / topics in deep learning.* https://iq.opengenus.org/key-terms-in-deep-learning/

22. Opten, O. (2023) *Understanding machine learning - The foundation of artificial intelligence.* https://vocal.media/futurism/understanding-machine-learning

23. Oxford University. (2022). *AI is the new Electricity - Meet the new power generation.* https://www.oxford.ai/

REFERENCES

24. Panka Psychology (2023) *Psychology of Chat GPT AI source work analysis.* https://pankajpsychology.com/chat-gpt-ai-source-info-work-investors/

25. Perri, L. (2022) *What's new in the 2022 Gartner hype cycle for emerging technologies.* Gartner. https://www.gartner.com/en/articles/what-s-new-in-the-2022-gartner-hype-cycle-for-emerging-technologies

26. Phan, T., Rieger, M. and Wang, M. (2018). *Segmentation of financial clients by attitudes and behavior: A comparison between Switzerland and Vietnam.* https://www.researchgate.net/publication/328329114_Segmentation_of_financial_clients_by_attitudes_and_behavior_A_comparison_between_Switzerland_and_Vietnam

27. Ridzuan. (2023) *Natural language processing with deep learning.* https://deeplearningmy.com/natural-language-processing-with-deep-learning/

28. Robles, B. (2023) *ChatGPT and use cases: The rise of AI technology in analytics.* https://www.uxax.org/post/chat-gpt-and-use-cases-the-rise-of-ai-technology-in-analytics

29. Rohit, S. (2019) *Top 8 machine learning frameworks every data scientist should know about.* https://www.upgrad.com/blog/machine-learning-frameworks/

30. Russel, S.J. and Norvig, P. (2021) *Artificial intelligence: a modern approach.* 4th ed. Hoboken, Pearson.

REFERENCES

31. Seismic. (n.d.) *White Paper: Preparing for AI-guided selling: A roadmap for forward-thinking businesses.* https://www.b2saas.com/uploads/topics/files/seismic/4.pdf

32. Sysdig. (n.d.) *What is multi-cloud security?* https://sysdig.com/learn-cloud-native/cloud-security/multi-cloud-security/

33. Techasoft. (2023) *Supervised vs. unsupervised learning in machine learning.* https://www.techasoft.com/post/supervised-vs-unsupervised-learning-in-machine-learning

34. The UK Time. (2022) *Marketing automation software: Upgrade your marketing strategy!* https://theuktime.com/marketing-automation-software/

35. Vogel, K. Ouagram-Gormley, S. (2022) *China's biomedical data hacking threat: Applying big data isn't as easy as it seems.* Texas National Security Review. https://tnsr.org/2022/04/chinas-biomedical-data-hacking-threat-applying-big-data-isnt-as-easy-as-it-seems/

ACKNOWLEDGEMENTS

I'd like to thank my husband, Howard, for the never-ending cups of tea and sage advice while I was writing this book. We've enjoyed many ideological discussions about Artificial Intelligence, which prompted me to delve further in my quest for the most useful information to include.

I'd also like to thank those people on LinkedIn who engage so whole-heartedly on the topic of AI and small business / solopreneurship. Keeping the enthusiasm alive has helped me to stay on course, convincing me that there was much good to be done with AI, if only we're armed with the right information.

But most of all, I'd like to thank you for buying this book. I hope that it helps you work out where to start on your AI journey, and what questions you need to ask.

Hopefully together we can shape this brave new world into one that brings AI-Powered Success to everyone.

ABOUT THE AUTHOR

Helen McCandless is a Senior Business Analyst, turned Author and Academic, who lives in Canberra, Australia with her family and pets amongst the visiting wildlife and birds.

Helen has had a long-standing relationship with IT, spanning over the past 20+ years, involved mostly with helping business owners make informed choices about new technology products.

If you'd like discuss a possible collaboration or speaking opportunity about AI in small business, please contact her at:

helen@balabaustralia.com

Made in United States
North Haven, CT
05 November 2026

21768321R10115